Stay In The Drain

OLIVER KELLEHER

STAY IN THE DRAIN

Oliver Kelleher

Published in Ireland in 2023

Design and layout:
SiobhanFoody.com

ISBN 978-1914596-19-3

Contents

Introducing
Oliver Kelleher

Oliver Kelleher was born in the parish of Gortletteragh outside Mohill, Co Leitrim in the west of Ireland. It's the biggest parish in Leitrim. It is known for having the best and most fertile land in Ireland for growing whins, nettles, bauhalans better known as ragwort and weeds. In another era his neighbour was the biggest farmer in Ireland. Lord Leitrim, who once lived in Lough Rynn Estate down the road from him, was the biggest landowner in Ireland with a few plots of land amounting to 63,000 acres in Donegal, Kildare and Leitrim.

From an early age Oliver showed signs of his entrepreneurial talents. At seven years of age, he used to collect the old age pension for Odie Clyne, a homeboy who came to live and work on their farm. Every Friday he collected the pension for Odie at the local post office. On the way home he drank half the pension.

Having left the national school, he was bundled off to a boarding school in Cavan to make a priest out of him. It didn't happen. It wasn't meant to be because it was his mother who had the vocation. After doing his Leaving Cert he headed for the bright lights of Dublin to seek a fortune. His first job was a start on a building site. He stuck that for three months before starting as a trainee supermarket manager with Pat Quinn and his wife Ann, who had just returned from Canada to set up Quinnsworth.

He spent eight exciting years there and moved on after Quinnsworth was taken over. He always had the longing for the road and to become a commercial traveller. Since then, he has spent most of his natural life in this trade having set up his own business over four decades ago.

That was in Castlebar where he setup a hygiene and catering equipment business with his late wife Mary. Over the years the business expanded into trophies and awards, giftware, a fancy dress shop and a catering equipment hire business. The businesses are now run by his family.

Over the years Oliver has appeared on TV shows for some of his inventions which he designed and developed some years ago. One was a glass that holds the head on beers and lagers. He also designed and developed a tabletop cooking unit for restaurants. He showed his talent for cooking when he took part and came runner-up on a RTÉ cookery programme. His fans have regularly told him he was 'robbed' out of winning. For over six years he wrote a popular opinion column for *The Connaught Telegraph* and the *Western People*.

Oliver now spends his time writing and dealing on the stock market. He has become an expert on the art of making a small fortune and losing a small fortune in stocks and shares. Like farming, 'some days are diamonds, and some days are stone'.

You could get a call from Oliver from any part of the world. From doing business in Hong Kong to looking up his famous neighbours in Tasmania or travelling around Australia or New Zealand or in Fidel Castro's Cuba or building houses in Cape Town with the Niall Mellon Township Trust or cooking boxty at the heritage days in Castlebar or playing a blinder on a reality cooking show on RTÉ or selling his bar and catering equipment on the highways and by-ways around Ireland.

Despite all his travels, he never lost touch with his home county of Leitrim or his adopted county of Mayo where he sponsored many sporting events and many charity events and fundraisers.

In this book Oliver gives a hilarious account of the ups and downs he has had in life. He can remember most of the ups and doesn't want to remember any of the downs. A question he is often asked is, 'If you had your life to live all over again, what would you do'. His answer is always the same, 'I would live my life all over again'. A good way to look at life.

It's a good read that will give you plenty of laughs and things to think about.

Acknowledgements

FIRSTLY, I got the inspiration to write this book after I did an interview with Michael Commins on Midwest Radio over 33 years ago, after he asked one personal question about how I did in my Leaving Cert.

So, I told him the story and the punchline stayed with me.

I did the Leaving in 1966 and my results came that September. At the time my results came I was down the field in Leitrim digging a drain in a swamp. I saw my father at the top of the hill and he had a brown envelope in his hand. I knew there was trouble coming. He shouted down at me, 'your Leaving Cert results came'.

I said to him, 'how did I do?'

He shouted back to me, 'stay in the drain!'

Thirty years on from that interview, I still meet people who ask me the same question, 'Are ya still in the drain?'

So, I want to thank Michael Commins and all the listeners of Midwest who were listening on that night. Every time I meet Michael, it reminds me of the slavery I went through in life, starting off digging drains on our land trying to get water to flow up hills, down hills and out of our rush filled fields where the swans and seagulls needed wellingtons to land in and take off. With these types of conversations, I was regularly asked, 'When are you going to write a book?'

I had to take the plunge and get it off my chest and get all my fans off my back.

I'm dedicating this book to all these people who gave me the inspiration. To all my friends and family who put up with me over the years and to all our customers and staff who had faith in me and my businesses over the last 45 years.

I would like to thank David Brennan and Edwin McGreal in Mayo Books Press for all their assistance in getting the book published and to the book's designer, Siobhan Foody for all her work.

And to you, the people who buy the book, borrow the book or steal it from a friend and read it, I hope you enjoy it as much as I enjoyed researching and writing it.

Again, I appreciate your support and inspiration you gave me to put pen to paper to write my memoirs.

Finally, I want to remember those who went before us. Many people mentioned in this book have since gone to their eternal reward. May they rest in peace.

Chapter 1

Stay in the drain

Growing up on a farm in Leitrim was a huge disadvantage as against growing up in any other county. Most parts of south Leitrim had good land, bad land, bogs, streams, rivers and beautiful lakes. The greatest concern my parents had was if there was an animal stuck in a drain, was the ass on the road or were the sheep stuck in briars in the fort?

The fort was a sacred place on our farm. Unknown territory because we weren't allowed to go there, it was sacred, stay away. Most of our land was unworkable because it was made up of hills you sometimes had to climb on your belly, like climbing a steep mountain. I broke the handle of every shovel and spade trying to dig a field of stones. The handle was probably rotten from being left up against a wall outside instead of being left inside in a shed. We envied everyone from Meath and the midlands. They had everything. They had green grass and limestone land, we had whins, bushes, bad roads, thieving cattle, sheep, asses and ponies.

The first little pony we got was one we bought from a traveller. The pony certainly was a traveller too. Two days after we bought him, he disappeared. He got homesick so he headed back home through the fields. My father spent half his life searching for cattle, sheep, ponies or me. He was told one time by a horse dealer that the best thing to do when you buy a pony is to put him into a field with other animals and birds and he will live happily then after that. That didn't happen so Fonsi headed off. The best approach at the time of purchase was to bring the pony home, put him into the neighbour's field and Fonsi will break into our field and make that his home. It didn't work because we could never catch him. He could see us coming to get him. He would take off like a jumbo jet and jump a wall twice his own height.

When it rained, around our house was like an island on top of a hill. You looked out the bedroom window in the morning and you were surrounded by water. Wellingtons were in big demand in every house. Money was scarce. There was no shame in being poor, it was just the inconvenience of it. We were all in the same boat in every way.

Jimmy Lennon came around to buy hens from us. He was a small little man with a limp in his leg. He had a stutter as well. He said the same words a few times before he got the full sentence out. He didn't need to say the whole sentence because you knew what he was saying even when his lips weren't moving. He always had a way of downgrading your hen. She either had 'bandy' legs or a crooked breast. He would say, 'I'm sorry Mrs Kelleher, she has kkkooked breast' and then he became the dragon in the den. He would offer you half of what you were asking. A row would start so he would up the price a bit and the deal was done and he walked away with a few prized hens.

The hen would have to have a very crooked breast or very bandy legs before he would declare himself out. My father would have worse luck with the cattle at the fair. I would walk the cattle the five miles to Mohill. This training stood to me for the rest of my life. I became a sprinter, a long-distance runner and a high jumper from trying to stop cattle running into neighbour's fields that had a bush in the gap instead of a gate. Some of these animals were a bit wild. They would still jump the gate if there was one there. I had to jump the gate or the wall after them or miss John Whelahan at the fair. John and Pat Whelahan were big buyers of cattle. As soon as John appeared on the Fair Green in Mohill he was sur-rounded by farmers who were hoping he would buy the lot from them. John was a good catch with money. He used to say that fellas would promise him the sun, moon and stars if he did the deal and bought the five or six cattle they had at the fair. The only problem John said was you had to collect the sun, moon and stars yourself. He inspected them if you had three or four animals. They would do the deal for the lot and I could head downtown for a good roast beef dinner with the full monty of carrots, parsnips, onions and Bisto gravy. That fortified me for the day. My father would go for a few bottles of stout and meet up with other farmers. He didn't know when to come home.

Next day it was back to pulling weeds, picking stones and cutting bushes to put in the gap. Then it was down the fields to pull the boholans (ragwort) that seemed to grow everywhere. I hadn't a great record at growing useful stuff like avocados, bananas or pears. All I had to do was to look at a nettle or a weed and it was in full bloom within days. My mother used to make nettle soup. We were told it was full of iron and was good for you. She used to mix it with cabbage to hoodwink us into thinking it was all cabbage. It didn't do us any harm. To this day I still make nettle soup in my gourmet kitchen. When I don't tell guests what the soup is made from, they tell me it's gorgeous with a dollop of cream with a few herbs and spices. Something like you get in some Michelin star restaurants nowadays.

Chapter 2

The long acre and the wandering pony

John Conboy sat beside me for two years in national school. John's only interest in life was Connemara ponies, asses and horny ewes (which were young sheep with horns). Even though he had no land, he had stock on the long acre. Oftentimes there was more grass on the long acre (which was grazing along the road) than there was in the fields. Conboy had a field under his house which was flooded for four months of the year by the Rynn river. During that period, he specialised in rearing swans, seagulls, and more exotic birds you couldn't eat because you couldn't catch them.

John spent most of his time in or around Foxe's pub keeping all the neighbours up to date on the happenings in the neighbourhood and further. He wasn't great at school because he didn't spend long enough there. His spelling wasn't great because he was a slow writer. He wasn't very slow when it came to counting money or selling horny ewes.

He had a horny ewe who would attack everything that moved above the grass. If you weren't careful and he came up behind you, he would give you a right root up the whole of your spine. There was little money in sheep or asses then but regardless of what John got, it was a bonus because the cost of feed was zero. If you use the long acre today and a car hit one of your horny ewes, it will cost you dearly in payouts and fines.

Having been reared on the land you always have an affiliation with cattle, crops and nature. Having moved from 65 acres in Leitrim to eventually settling on a half-acre in Mayo, the longing was always there to return to the land. The grass got a bit overgrown on my land in Castlebar, so I bought a mini pony at a fair in Ballaghaderreen for £400 to mow my grass instead of paying £400 for a lawnmower. Disaster struck from day one. Nelly was on her own

on the land. No female or male company. I was told this could be
a disaster because like ourselves, ponies get lonesome and long for
a bit of company, male or female.

From day one he too was a wanderer because he took to the
road, and he was impossible to corner even if six of us surrounded
him. Eventually I got him well fenced in with a little shed and
plenty of nuts and hay. He still wasn't happy because when I left
the back kitchen door open, he would come in, raid any food he
could get his mouth on and sleep on the floor. I hit another stumbling block when the pony was inside the fence and some concerned passer-by phoned the animal rights department to say I
had a pony that was being neglected because he was out in the rain,
even though he had his own little home to go to.

I wonder would the passerby be as concerned if they saw a person homeless, as is sadly often the case these days.

After several complaints from the concerned animal welfare
lover, several calls from the welfare officer, Nelly had to find
another home even though I had shown the welfare officer photos
of Nelly at the kitchen table eating a dinner of chicken, peas and
mash which he snared off the table onto the floor when my back
was turned. He went to live with a family of sheep, horses, cows
and bullocks outside Swinford. He still has a great memory. Despite the fact that we parted on good terms, I called to see how he
was getting on. As soon as he saw my face at the top of the field, he
took off like a jumbo jet taking off at Knock airport. When I had
him, the only way I could catch him was to lasso him like John
Wayne in the cowboy films. Nelly had a good memory, after four
or five years. He was happy and he didn't want to end up all alone
in this big bad world. Would you blame him?

Chapter 3

Growing up in Leitrim was a treat

Growing up anywhere you have good friends is a treat. There are things that happen that you never forget or want to forget. There are people you knew and liked and you never wanted to lose touch with and there were a few you wanted to see the back of like the fella who fired a duster with a wooden back on it from behind the class. There were the bucks who didn't like you. There were the women you fancied but never got a chance to tell them until 40 years later when it was too late. There were the teachers who should have given me a 'clip' when it was well deserved but they didn't. There were the fearful times when the doctor or the dentist were doing their rounds.

Being from Leitrim you were sort of seen as having a bit of an impediment. I soon found out this when I went to boarding school to become a priest. Leitrim was classed as the poorest county in Ireland even though my neighbour of another era was the biggest landowner in Ireland. Lord Leitrim, who resided in Lough Rynn, had over 63,000 acres spread out between Donegal, Leitrim and Kildare. In secondary boarding school we all got a tag. I went to boarding school in Cavan. We all got tags the first day depending on where you came from. The boys from Mullahoran on the Longford border were often referred to as the Mullahungers because they would eat all around them.

Their main topic of conversation was Danny or Phil 'The Gunner' Brady who played for Cavan or John Joe Reilly who captained the Cavan team when they won the All-Ireland in New York in 1947. John Joe Reilly was from Cornafean but everyone wanted to claim him just like everyone wanted to claim Charlie Haughey when he was in his prime. He was a Mayo man, a Kerry man, remember Inishvickillane and a Dublin man when it came to politics.

Boarding school is not for everyone. It was fine for me because I got away from doing the things in Leitrim I hated. Digging drains, shoring, pulling whins and baulahans and nettles and dead end jobs that there was no money in unless you could sell nettle soup to Irish returned emigrants who wanted something hot and different. I fell into a pile of nettles one time and I ended up with a face that looked like overcooked crinkle cup pumpkins.

Being teased about my Leitrim upbringing never bothered me though. In many ways, it was the life I wanted and enjoyed.

To the others it was the life they never knew, being reared in a house with no back garden, no front garden or no running water in the fields around your house. To me, at times, I felt at a disadvantage because I needed Odie or a neighbour to bring me to town just to stand on the street corner like the townies watching young women passing. At that time, you could whistle at them and get a whistle, a nod or a wink back. All harmless stuff.

In secondary school I was forced to listen to taunts from Cavan men about how we never won an All-Ireland in Leitrim. They had one up on me and they still dream to this day of lining out in Croke Park like John Joe Reilly did in New York in 1947.

Later in life I studied the counties who won several All-Ireland titles. Who had the most? Two counties I was most impressed with won 38 All-Ireland titles between them. Very few could name the two, Leitrim and Kerry have 38 titles between them. I was challenged a few times on this, and I stuck to my words. So, how did Kerry and Leitrim come to have 38 All-Ireland senior football titles between them? Simple, Kerry has 38 and Leitrim have none. Answer to the quiz.

I'm often told Leitrim didn't get its first set of traffic lights until the late 1980s. True. They didn't need them. You only fit traffic lights when you cannot control traffic and traffic lights are then an excuse to make excuses for traffic jams. Traffic lights are now part of traffic control in many places even though proper pedestrian crossings in city centres and big towns are a much more effective way of controlling traffic and giving pedestrians use of roads they are entitled to cross in comfort. Modern apps and technology say different, and I won't argue with technology. It's a war you cannot win even when you are right.

Today Leitrim is one of the most sought-after destinations for fishing, boating, cruising and relaxing. It's a place where they still appreciate their heritage and culture. Like most parts of the west of Ireland. They still say hello, goodbye and thank you in restaurants, bars and businesses. It's classed a bit odd at times, people saying hello to you on the street. All of this is part of what you are and if you get slagged off or laughed about your personality it's a plus and a pleasure. Enjoy it while it lasts.

At the end of our road lived Willie and Kate. Kate was called 'the doll'. She was a small little woman like a doll. I used to turn the hay for them. No money, I was just fed. You wouldn't class it as gourmet food. A few slices of bread and a scrape of butter, maybe margarine and tea out of a stained mug with a few chips gone out of it. If the fox hadn't taken the three hens she had, you might get an egg. No caviar sandwiches or honey and mustard roasted ham.

They lived a prudent life. I'm told when they passed away many years ago, they found money stuffed everywhere and buried in tins in the garden. I don't think there were millions there. Maybe a hundred pounds or less.

Kate was a shrewd little woman with the money even though they had little outgoings as they had no family. A story was once told that Kate employed a labourer to do work around the house. She had some dispute with him, so she didn't pay for the work. The man called a few times to collect the money, but nothing was forthcoming. On his last visit, there was a neighbour of Kate's in the house. She had run to the room. Before he left, he said he would be back dead or alive for the money. Kate heard the words from the room, ran down, took ten bob out of a drawer and ran him before he put a curse on her.

Kate honestly believed he had the power to collect his money dead or alive. I don't think that has ever happened where someone came back to collect their money after they died.

Chapter 4

My school days and violence in the classroom

There was violence in every school when I was growing up. You were liable to get a kick in the arse or a clip on the ear from your mates. If it wasn't someone lobbing a duster or a book from the bottom of the class, it was the teacher giving out slaps to a few who were giving 'lip'.

Our school was no different even though I was seldom at the 'butt' end of the cane. I knew when to talk and when to shut up and when to listen. In fairness most of the teachers I had in national school were 'civilised' and they only used the cane when all other methods of 'coaxing' and 'negotiating' had failed.

Most of the violence for me started when the dentist arrived at the school to pull teeth. You were lined up like cattle at the fair in Mohill for the job. There was no counselling, no forward planning meetings with the victim. The dentist was there. There was a job to be done. Whether he pulled one or four teeth wasn't an issue for him but it was an issue with me.

I was called up and planked in the chair. They stuck a wire sort of frame into your mouth so you couldn't open your mouth or roar. They then injected your gums with 'ether' which tasted like peppermint sweets. That was the only nice thing about it.

The dentist decided to shift at least one tooth at the back. When I saw the big needle swirling in his hand, I decided I had enough of this crap. When the dentist turned his back, I got up to go. He went for me to try to relax me. By then I had drawn a kick on him and hit him on the shin bone. I escaped out the back door into the yard over the six foot wall and down the field home. To this day I still have that tooth and it hasn't caused me too much bother.

That was just one of the few things I abhorred about school. I

often hear horror stories about teachers sending pupils out into
the field to cut a 'plant', a blackthorn stick and bring it back so the
teacher could batter him with it. I heard another story where a
teacher used to catch an unruly buck by the ears, lift him up and
say, 'Do you see heaven'? Anything was possible there because of
how the system worked.

It wasn't just in schools where things happened that should not
have happened. There was no point blaming the teachers because
they were told to do this to keep control. It was the politicians who
put these systems there, helped on by the Catholic Church and, in
some cases, condoned by parents of children. That was the system,
and in most cases, people could write their own rules.

The same thing still applies where people write their own rules,
and they are let because politicians and regulators don't want to
rock the boat especially where big business applies their own rules
and regulations.

I got into bother now and again at school. It was mainly because
of the answers I gave or didn't give. I nearly always had an answer.
It mightn't be the right answer but at least it was an answer.

One day Master Crossan asked me which was the furthest away,
the moon or America. 'America' I said. 'How do you work that
out?' 'Well', I said, 'I can see the moon and I can't see America.'

Master Crossan started his first teaching job in our school. It
was a baptism of fire for him until he got to know us. He was one
of our own, a real gentleman who would advise you on the best
path in life to take provided there was a path that was suited to me.

John Bohan would be asked to spell out three fruits and vegetables starting with a 'n'.

A napple, a norange and a nonion he would give as the answer.
'Stand in the corner.'

Master Crossan never used the cane. He was probably afraid of
us half hooligans from the border county who were supposed to
be somewhat uncivilised.

We always had the answers. John Reynolds was asked to spell
paint. He didn't know how to spell it, so he took it one step further
by asking 'what colour Sir?'

There was an English lad in our class who had a very cultured
English accent. There was a question on wild animals.

The teacher asked him, 'Ivan, what is a bison?'

'It's what you wash your face in.' In a way we were all geniuses, but we didn't know it.

John Bohan was the tallest fella in my class in school. He was nearly six foot when he left national school. He is still a big, hardy man. He owes a lot of his physique to me. At school he used to fancy my mother's Michelin Star cooking.

Regularly, I would share my boxty and bonnach with him in return for his mother's current bread. My mother cooked boxty regularly for us. Bonnach was a treat because it was a tedious job mixing oatmeal, flour, water, salt and pepper, mixing it, rolling it out and putting it on a big horseshoe shape grill in front of the fire and turning it every five minutes until it was baked into a hard substance like Ryvita which you ate with the side teeth because it was so hard it would break you front teeth if you tried eating it like bread.

Bonnach originated in Newfoundland, probably by the Irish on their way to America. It was a very sustainable food which would stay fresh for months or years provided it was kept dry. My grandmother used to tell me the Irish always brought a supply with them wrapped in paper in a tin canister to keep them from starving on the journey to America. I believe in olden days fishermen from Newfoundland brought it with them to sea for the term they would spend at sea. This was part of the art of survival in an era when we had no apps or technology.

School then is a bit different than today. You went to school then to meet all your friends and get away from pulling weeds and picking stones in Leitrim. As soon as you picked one stone another appeared. After a week you could have a huge pile built up in the corner of the field. They were useless. You couldn't burn them, eat them or build anything with them because they were either round or too small. If you happened to be an unfortunate person who was transported to Van Diemen's Land some years ago you would be given the same job to do every day.

Chapter 5

Drinking the pension

Getting me to go to school was a battle. Getting to school was another battle and trying to stay in my seat and learn things was a bigger battle. We lived two and a half miles from the school by road but across the fields it was a mile. I took off up the lane, up the hills, down the hills, through drains, bushes, whines and briars. The blood could be running out of my hands by the time I got to the school. No sympathy in those days. The teacher might say 'You'll know better the next time not to be climbing trees'.

On the way back by road, I passed four neighbour's houses. The first was my auntie, Mary. She made lovely scones and brown bread hot out of the Stanley range. The butter melted on it in seconds and the butter ran down your lips while you downed it.

Going to school was a challenge. It was never my thing. To me it was a waste of good time where I could be doing other things that would create a small income to keep me in the lifestyle I had become accustomed to. To many of my friend's school was a distraction. At 16 some of them went to work in England in the trenches or in the tunnels. That wasn't for me. I had seen enough of the feckin' stuff already.

My mother was an early riser and she called me first to milk the cows before I got my lunch ready with whatever was left in the house before I headed to the church to serve Mass and from there onto school. On these mornings I had to get up at half seven in the morning. It took me a while to realise there was a half seven in the morning as well as half seven in the evening.

Before I started my academic career, I had a great few years with plenty of money in my pocket to buy any of the things in life most six or seven year olds only dream of. Just a month after I came into this world my father took on a 'homeboy' to work on the farm. Odie, the 'homeboy', was reared in an orphan's home. At the time I used to ask my mother why he was reared in an orphan's home.

I never got a straight answer.

From an early age he was my minder because I was there in a cot roaring my head off to get fed or be taken out of the cot. He had to use all his skills to settle me. It was a battle and still is to this day. Odie had arthritis. He couldn't walk without the aid of two sticks. As I got older and wiser, I knew Odie had a bit of money, more money than the rest of us as he got the pension every week.

When I got to the use of reason, I collected the pension every Friday for him. Five shillings was the amount, about 26c in today's money. You could buy a lot of things with five shillings that time. Fianna Fáil were in power then. They didn't know what inflation meant then. They weren't long learning because better the lot of them in Fianna Fáil, Fine Gael, Labour, the Greens, excluding Sinn Fein, haven't stopped taxing us since. In fairness Sinn Fein have promised they will give it all back. That's called 'repentance'.

I repented several times only to break my own rules when it suited me. I always had Odie's money when I was growing up. I minded it for him. His pension was the most lucrative financial deal. When I collected the five shillings, I went on a drinking spree at seven years of age. Cidona, Lucozade and Club orange were my favourites when I collected his pension. I then headed to my school friends' houses, and we drank the lot. Tired and sick from all I drank, I headed for home and deposited a half a crown, half the pension, in Odie's secure jam pot. He never complained about being short changed. I could do no wrong and I never did. Some thieving bastards would bring him back nothing. Odie had come to us to work for three months. He died in our house 13 years later. How he ended up with us was a friend of my father's, Jack Nichol was a returned yank who had spent six months in America. He came back, bought a farm and took on Odie as a farm worker.

Jack decided that the opportunities in New York were better than pulling weeds and picking stones on 30 acres in Leitrim. He asked my father if he would take Odie on to work on our farm for three months as he had to go back to New York to sort out some issues. He didn't come back and Odie remained in our house for 13 years instead of three months.

Nichol came back from America with a Yankee twang as if he were there all his life. He bought a couple of farms that snipes and swans would need to wear wellingtons to get around. Between jobbing in calves and lectures on the opportunities in America, he spent the rest of his life on the 30 acres, most of the time spent cutting rushes and whines and trying to grow a few potatoes and vegetables to feed a family.

It was never my scene. I used to cringe at the sight of my father down the fields doing stuff they did 200 years ago long before Fianna Fáil or Fine Gael were even heard of. When they did come on the scene it obviously gave a new lease of life, a new way of thinking for those downtrodden people who had been ruled by the British for over 800 years.

We are now living in the land of milk, honey and roses. We are good at producing all of these with or without the politicians. We still need politicians to tell us what to do and how to do it arseways. We still need politicians to put policies in place, collect taxes and squander it on consultants, experts and free legal aid to people who own multiple properties, high powered cars and Rolex watches who didn't have a meaningful job to pay legal eagles to defend them. It's a sad world when we cannot look after everyone in society.

Chapter 6

Surviving on the farm

Farming in Leitrim was a trial and error set up. You had more errors than trials. It was a bit like the stock market. Today, cattle prices were up, tomorrow, they were down, well down. That's why you never met a farmer who would tell you he was doing well. Women farmers will tell you as it is.

Now and again, I would meet a neighbour who had a good farm. I would make the comment to him, 'You're cleaning up'.

'I am every morning cleaning the cow dung out of the cowshed,' he replied.

Today and then, that was a valuable commodity for gardening, the best of organic stuff.

It wasn't a fancy job, but someone had to do it and it was usually me who obliged. I'd have to spend a half hour washing myself before I headed off to serve Mass and onto school.

Farming could be a disaster of a business to be in. You had to contend with the weather, the flooding, crops failing, potatoes being hit by the blight and predators like the ones that wait for things to ripen and then they pounce. If it wasn't the rats, it was the crows.

The rats would attack the potato heap in the field and the crows would attack the oats we had in the shed to feed the hens. The following week the fox would have taken a couple of hens. The magpies would bring the eggs when the hens started to lay out under a bush. My father would go mad. He would be upstairs with the shotgun out the window waiting for some of these thieving bastards to round the corner at the bottom of the hill. He might have fired 20 shots, but I don't think he ever connected. They were all too cute for him, they saw him in the window. Wouldn't you be. On one occasion he shot two of the hens instead of the crows. My father always called a spade a spade except when he tripped over one. That's when the row might start, who left the spade hanging on the ground for him to fall over. There was never a culprit. He should have seen it even in the dark, that was my approach.

At least one thing about the farm was it was never boring even though you often took your life in your hands. A young bullock might give you a puck across the head that could knock all your brains out. That's why you need to keep 'your head about you' to survive on the farm or in the cow shed.

We knew all our neighbours and a lot of those across the border in Longford. Some you knew for good reasons and others for the wrong reasons. Some of them started their working life in England, drinking and fighting in the pubs. We knew them all, even the ones who lived five or six miles away from us.

My father spent a few years in England. He never got into the fighting scene. He was too small even to defend himself, so he always took the negotiating route. He got a black eye once when he was trying to settle a row. One buck turned on him and landed him. His explanation at the time was, 'I should have been listening when I was talking'.

Some of the hardy bucks my mother often referred to as 'pure haverals'. This could have a double meaning. It could describe a fella who was six feet four in height, 20 stone weight who could lift the back of a Morris Minor with the back wheel spinning. The other could be a sort of a BIFFO (a big ignorant fucker from Offaly) or BIFFL (the Leitrim version), because he was as thick as an ass even though an ass is a gentle creature nowadays. Some of them learned faster than their human owners of today.

Many of our neighbours were Church of Ireland or Protestants, as we only knew them as. They were the best of neighbours. I never heard of religious bigotry until the Troubles started in the North. Obviously, it was there for years but only came to light when Catholics in the North were getting a rawer deal than their Protestants counterparts. This happened because of the political system that prevailed everywhere, not just in the North. Depending on your colour, creed or religion you could become a victim of the systems which are run by politicians and civil servants.

Our Protestant neighbours had as much money or as little money as we had because a Protestant field would grow nettles, bohalouns and weeds the same as a Catholic field. Regularly our cattle could get stuck in a drain between our land and Benny Lloyd's land. Benny would come to help. He never asked if the bullock was a Catholic bullock or a Protestant bullock.

The Peace Process has brought us back to those years and that thinking in most parts of Ireland. Why did the Catholics and Protestants politicians not see this years beforehand? Ego, power and money can be the cause of many of the issues in the world. If you took politicians and religion out of things it might be easier to find solutions. Maybe not.

A visit to the 'azoo', as we called Dublin Zoo, was always a treat. It still is. Dublin was the 'in' place then. You had to get to Dublin before you reached the use of reason. We went on Ned Maguire's bus to the zoo, 20 of us. The master bought the tickets which included a drink in a red plastic cup and a sandwich made with butter and ham. None of the boring rabbit food you get nowadays like lettuce, carrots, cucumber and a host of flavoured mayo, ketchup or dips. You didn't need an ID to get into the zoo. One fella who looked, dressed and acted the monkey most of the time nearly had to produce ID to get out.

The zoo hasn't changed much since then, you still see the same elephants lazing around with big arses and not able to get up because of being too well fed or from pure laziness. The monkeys have not changed much. They have become cuter if anything. They grabbed the sandwich out of one of my school pal's hands. He mustn't have been too fond of ham sandwiches because he threw it back at him and ran over to have fun with one of his female friends while rubbing his arse with his bare hand.

We have people around the world who are for and against locking wild animals behind a big wire fence. The same people have issues with circuses using elephants and wild animals, so we can feed them bread we are told is bad for them while it is perfect for you and me to eat. Strange world.

The only difference between these monkeys and ordinary family pets like cats and dogs is when they meet, they start to smell one another's arses, while humans smile and say hello to one another. With modern technology this is beginning to change. Let's hope that we don't go down the cats and dogs' route yet. I don't want us all to end up in the zoo.

Chapter 7

Homeboys and how they coped

In the early part of the 1900s there was homelessness and displaced people in Ireland like there is today. Some lived in makeshift hovels, under canvas or in houses built from mud with thatch on them. It was a roof over their heads, no more. As time moved on houses were being built with dry stone with walls two feet thick. They were nearly soundproof and waterproof. You heated them with a big turf fire and hot water bottles in the bed. In the cities they had a similar life with less of the 'goodies' in life.

In the country you had a few acres to grow vegetables, potatoes and many of the basic foods you could grow easily using organic manure like the cow dung, horse dung or waste vegetation that rotted. If you had hens, chicks or pigs you would never go hungry or be malnourished.

Most farmhouses with over 50 acres had a 'homeboy' at one stage or another. They were a bit like modern day 'refugees' whom the decent people of Ireland gave a break to. Some of these were good, conscientious, honest workers who became part of the family. Many homeboys like Odie were not physically fit to work because of arthritis or stiffness in the bones from the winter cold. More of them had no interest in work and more of them would sleep beside it. Horses for courses as they say.

In the 1960s the 'homeboy' employment dried up because these people could hop on a boat and get work in the UK working for McAlpine or John Bull.

Once they settled in with other Paddies in England, their life changed. They could work hard, get good money and forget about the bad old days of being incarcerated in an industrial school and the stigma of it. These schools and homes which were run by Christian Brothers and nuns played a big part in housing and feeding vulnerable children when nobody else wanted them.

Today we are back in a similar but worse situation being part of the EU that dictated to us how many refugees we have to take in and house even though we have our own housing crisis. This is despite there being over 150,000 vacant homes in Ireland that could be utilised within months. There's a great opportunity for people to take a common sense approach to these things rather than having meetings about meetings.

If we can't do it, the EU should put a plan in place to fast track a housing development plan to handle 100,000 houses in the next year. It's possible and doable if you can plan it.

For now, we can only talk about it and dream about it. For the people who are badly affected by it, those who arrive at our airports and are forced to sleep in a corridor or a staircase – that is not the answer to anything. Trying to make things work, even simple things, can be a challenge in good times or bad times. It's the way you put the plan in place that makes things happen.

The first homeboy who came to work on our ranch was from Dublin. He had been released from Mountjoy prison after spending a couple of years there for robbery. The authorities probably felt as a last resort a new start in life the country life would settle him.

He arrived in Longford by train. My father collected him, we had a car at that time. He wasn't too fond of work or the country life. After two weeks he was gone one morning but not before he stole my mother's engagement ring. It was said he was courting a woman in Mohill and he got engaged to her using my mother's engagement ring. At least we gave him the start, a good start in life and to marriage.

He didn't invite my mother or father to the wedding. I'm not sure if they would have any reason to go other than to retrieve the stolen engagement ring. I don't know if my mother ever replaced it. Like everything in life, you only get one chance to make a first impression and one may be one too many if it's the wrong impression you make.

Homeboys played a part in Ireland, mainly on farms in rural Ireland. Many of them had a good life and blended in with the family they went to work and live with. Odie had a great time. When he arrived in our house, he was given a bedroom on his own even though there were eight in our house with just three bedrooms, a kitchen and a sitting room we never sat in only when our relations came to visit on a Sunday. The China tea set would come out and they all got tea. We never drank coffee; it was too expensive. We had the odd garden party in the summer where my mother made currant bread or treacle bread for the guests. If there was some left over after the feast, we got it.

Today, the homeboys live a different life. If you were reared in an orphanage or in an industrial school, you were automatically assumed to be neglected or mistreated, and you are entitled to compensation. I knew a few of these people who never looked for compensation but were told they were entitled to money even though they were well treated in the places they were forced to go.

Some of them got jobs as soon as they left these places. Just like the system in the past there was always someone out there who was prepared to give a homeboy a chance in life, which we all need to get in life. Most of the nuns and brothers who ran these 'terrible' places had a heart and worked to give them a start in life.

Sadly, in modern times all of these people are 'tarred' the same. We are led to believe they were heartless people who, to this day, are often afraid to wear the clothing that represents their vocation because of the fear of being attacked verbally in the streets by ignorant people who have little respect for anyone, even themselves.

Chapter 8

The inconvenience of being poor

For many people in any part of the world growing up, living life, surviving in life can be a challenge. If you're born wealthy, you may find it hard to handle money or know the value of money. Money/wealth is one of the most debated subjects of conversation for generations. We envied the people who had any amount of money to do the things in life you want to do. It's not everyone's cup of tea because a lot of people like a challenge so we have things to look forward to. The pleasure we get from achieving things and being successful can more than outweigh the excitement you get from having a rich mammy and daddy.

Today rich mammies and daddies make a big difference to banks and other businesses. In the past twenty years the MAD bank has become part of the bank bailout. When your son or daughter want to buy or build a new home, they may be short for the deposit. That's where the MAD bank, the bank of Mam and Dad, comes into play. It was never part of my life because my parents were never in a position to bail me or the banks. Their main concern was giving us a good start in life and to have respect for everyone and do a good day's work. This was a good start. You either learned from your parents and it stood to you, or you went with the flow and could have ended up going nowhere. In today's world computers, technology and apps can do many of these things for you at the touch of a button or two. It was a time when there was no shame in being poor. It was just the inconvenience of it.

Any big family in rural Ireland, especially the west, had parents that were under a lot of pressure and not just financially. If you already had a priest or a nun in the family, the pressure was there to continue the religious line in the family. For that reason, I was bundled off to boarding school to make a priest out of me. I can see how they saw a vocation in me because they had a battle to get me to go to school even to learn nothing. I thought when I was ten or eleven that I had a vocation. What appealed to me most was the fact that neighbours over the road had a daughter a nun and a son a monsignor in America.

He used to come home, hire a car and travel the country. He always had money because all his nephews could buy houses at a young age from the dollars he sent from America. That was the part that kind of appealed to me. The bottom line was it was my mother who had the vocation, not me. I still went to boarding school for five years. It was a great time playing basketball, handball and football and learning a few things that might stand to me in later life. I didn't have the go in me to sit down studying Latin and Greek and move on to a world where nobody would ever speak to me in Latin or Greek. If I had gone ahead, I would have been able to say the Latin Mass or advise Greek Orthodox folk how to have a good life. I mixed with all types of students. Some went on to be actors, other writers, other drunkards and others musicians.

Chapter 9
Waiting for the Leaving

When I was released, I was free to do what I wanted to do. If I got a good Leaving Cert, I could have got a job in the civil service or I could get a job in the guards even without the Leaving Cert. My father didn't like the idea of me joining the guards. He didn't like the guards. He got pulled one night for not having a light on his bike. He was lucky at the time to have a bike.

He said to me, 'why don't you go and get a decent job?' Well, I said, 'it's better than walking the streets', which I probably would have ended up doing every day. I left the college and headed back to the farm to give a 'dig out' before I launched myself into a well-paid cushy job where I could play golf, go on fishing trips and a few sick days thrown in every month. The civil service was the only place that offered jobs like that. The only problem was to get a job like that. You needed 'pull' to get even considered for a job like that and my father didn't have that. Nobody was too sure whether he was a Fianna Fáil man or a Fine Gael man even though he had relations in politics, or so he told us.

We seemed to have relations everywhere through marriage, drink or the fact that their dog pissed in our garden. At this stage I was going to have to plough my own furrow and go searching for a job, any job. If I got a good Leaving Cert result, I could go on to become a doctor, a dentist or a solicitor. The Leaving Cert results hindered this. I would have needed to get five honours in my Leaving Cert to make myself eligible to follow up any of these careers. It wasn't going to happen as I only sat one honours paper in the Leaving Cert.

In the meantime, I was incarcerated on the farm. I was back digging ditches, pulling weeds and trying to stop our cattle falling in and getting stuck in drains in the bog that weren't cleaned since Cromwell was here. The most depressing job was 'shoring'. To try and make anything out of bad land you had to drain it by 'shoring'. This was an intricate job.

Firstly, Joe Leogue, the shoring inspector, came out and gave you a plan and if you went by the plan, you got a grant provided you supported either Fianna Fáil or Fine Gael and you or all your family gave them a 'stroke' on the ballot paper at election time. If you were a dedicated, diehard Fianna Fáil man who knocked on doors for 'your man', you got the full grant. There were very few women in Fianna Fáil at the time and just a few more in Fine Gael. There were several more breakaway parties around then and over the years who had very little 'clout'.

The 'shoring' was a woeful job. It would bread your back, wreck your head and give you blisters on your hands and knees. You first lined up the string where you were going to plan the 'shore'. The shore would be about twelve or fourteen inches wide, which is about 350mm or 35cm in today's jargon. When completed you had a drain to take water out of the field which was 14' inches, 350mm or 35cm wide and 18' inches, 450mm or 45cm deep. Simple enough to work out in today's technological world. You needed a good spade, a good back and a good stomach for the job. You didn't need too many letters after your name or too many honour subjects in your Leaving Cert to do a job like this.

After three days of this torture, I was in the drain 'shoring' up to my arse in water and me with a hole in my wellingtons and the water mixed with dobe massaging my little toes. It was hell on earth for me, cursing and swearing and promising myself I would do any feckin' job in the world except shoring and cleaning drains.

And if that wasn't bad enough, there was more to follow. It was September and it was beginning to get cold, especially in wet drains. It was nearly midday as I looked up the field and saw my father at the top of the field with a brown envelope in one hand and a mug of tea in the other. I knew something was up. He shouted down to me, 'Your Leaving Cert results came'. 'How did I do?' I asked. 'Stay in the drain' was his reply.

Enough said.

I had had enough so I kissed the shovel goodbye, packed my case, kissed my mother goodbye, told my father where to stick my Leaving Cert results and I headed to the bright lights of Dublin.

Chapter 10

Dublin, Sorohans and Quinnsworth

I was lucky when I arrived in Dublin. I met one of the Sorohan brothers who had moved from Leitrim to build houses in the city. I got the start as a trainee block layer, come drain digger. I must have been an inspiration because Sorohan's Builders went on to build the best houses in Dublin. They won many awards for the quality of their houses and are still winning them to this day.

I was earning £20 a week and driving a £40 Renault Dauphine that would go through anything except a flood of water or even a pothole with water in it.

The money was good on the buildings but it wasn't going to be my life for the rest of my life. Like the ponies and sheep, we used to have, I wanted to 'break out' into greener pastures where you didn't have to break your back and have blisters on my dainty, little soft hands.

After six months another Leitrim man who had returned from Canada was setting up a supermarket in Ireland's first shopping centre in Stillorgan.

That year Pat Quinn opened the first Quinnsworth shop. I chanced my luck because I felt I would be good at dealing with people and looking after people.

With a 'bit of pull', I landed a job as a trainee manager starting on half the money Sorohan's paid me. Jim Quinn was an uncle of Pat Quinn's, and he was a cattle jobber from Longford. He did a bit of dealing in calves with my father. I got my father to put in a word to Jim to put in a word so I might get the job. It all worked out and I got the job, no interview, just arrived to work on the Monday morning and told you're starting now, get that coat off you.

From day one it was my career. I loved the work, the camaraderie and the simplicity of stacking shelves and remembering the price of everything in my head. We had no modern technology or apps to tell you, you had no mobile phones to contact someone when you were in trouble. I found it easy to pick things up because I loved the job and was interested. I read the instructions or the ingredients on every pack of flour or cereal. There were no metres, centimetres or millimetres then, just feet, inches and yards. Now we have all of that and we don't know any of them because we measure things in millimetres and then convert to inches.

Back in those days a lot of information was hit and miss. You didn't have Google or any other app to tell you about things. The only way was to read an encyclopaedia which would be like trying to read the Bible in a day. Talking about the Bible, in those years we had regular callers to our flat by people trying to convert us to God by reading the Bible more. One night one of these evangelists called to my door and handed me a leaflet and told me 'Jesus loves you'.

'Does he?' says I. 'He does,' says she. 'How do you know?' says I, 'were you talking to him?' It was the first time she was asked this question and obviously she didn't have the answer. You can now read this Bible on Kindle I presume and talk to God on Snapchat, Twitter and Facebook. He is a busy man trying to keep in touch with all of us on the planet.

Pat Quinn became a celebrity fast. He had been in the showbiz scene in Ireland and Canada running major events with bands like the Rolling Stones and others.

Back then he was a regular on The Late Late Show with his signature white polo neck shirt and his bald head. To me he was an inspiration to do the things in life you enjoy and you will be naturally good at. I more or less became part of the family. At 21 years old I was working in the supermarket as well as being a part-time chauffeur, collecting celebrities from airports and other places to bring to charity events the Quinns were sponsoring. I felt and looked a bit like a celebrity too, driving a Rolls Royce with my fancy suit, collar and tie. At that time, you wouldn't attempt to go out anywhere official without being togged out properly. Today the likes of Elon Musk, Jeff Bezos or Tim Cook give interviews and conduct company meetings with an open neck shirt, jeans or a tee shirt.

One of my first official drives was to collect a 'celebrity' from Dublin Airport and bring him to the Central Remedial Clinic which was run and funded by Lady Valerie Goulding, who was one of the Goulding fertiliser family. She was a lovely, pleasant lady whose only aim in life was to help people less fortunate than herself. The Quinn family were friends and sponsors of the clinic.

I got the call to collect someone at the airport. I hadn't a clue what he looked like. I just knew his name. I asked before I left what this fella looked like or how I would recognise him. I was told you will recognise him. He will have a head of long grey hair, pointed nose, flamboyant clothing and a big cigar in his mouth. I arrived at the airport, parked up my Rolls Royce and headed in. Within minutes I could see my man. He stood out from the crowd. He was none other than the infamous Jimmy Saville. He had come to Dublin to do some charity events in the Central Remedial Clinic.

While he made millions for many charities, including the Central Remedial Clinic, as we all found out, Jimmy Saville had a very different personality than what we saw on television. You'd have to wonder how it went on for so long and how so many people turned a blind eye to it.

I was living in the fast lane at the time, working in the food lanes in Quinnsworth and doing my driving in the evenings and at night. I would collect others from fancy restaurants where I could only afford to read the menu. I was driving famous men and women, managers of companies that supplied goods to Quinnsworth or the odd few who were neighbours of Pat Quinn when he was growing up in Cloone, Co Leitrim. He was one of their own. His father and six uncles came from Aughavas, up the road from Cloone. One weekend I got into a bit of bother with my £40 Renault Dauphine and I was planning to go to Leitrim for the weekend to play a match. Quinn, without hesitation, threw me the keys of his Rolls Royce. He told me not to hit too many ditches around Leitrim. I was in my glory. I was a new man at 21 years of age driving a Rolls Royce up and down the streets of Mohill, my arm out the window, whistling at everyone I knew. A friend of mine told me after that he heard someone on the street in Mohill say, 'Jasus will you look at Kelleher, he is only working in Quinnsworth a couple of years, and he is driving a Roller'.

In Dublin there was a guy who ran what I think was the first Michelin Star restaurant at the time. The story went out that it was fierce expensive and if you were a diner who complained about the food or the service, he would take the bill, tear it up and tell you to never come back again. We said we would give it a try. Myself and two of my mates booked it. We arrived in my Rolls Royce. When the bill arrived one of the bucks complained. Out comes the boss, listens to us for two minutes, takes the bill, tears it up and tells us to get out and never come back. We tried the same stunt a year down the road wearing fancy suits, sunglasses and a dickie bow. It didn't work, he recognised one of us from before even though it was an era when there was no CCTV, no hidden cameras or no smartphones to take our picture. Obviously, he didn't need them, he had a good memory. Seán Kinsella, the proprietor of the Mirabu Restaurant in Sandycove was a flamboyant character. His signature dish in the restaurant was roast duck and orange sauce. It was said that the main ingredient in the orange sauce was Little Chip marmalade and we never questioned that because it tasted good.

Eventually I had to kiss my Rolls Royce goodbye and start to make a decent living. I moved on to working on the road as a commercial traveller. This was the first time I had a new car under my arse with expenses thrown in. Most of my salary was made up of commission where you got paid on the amount of sales you got. That suited me because I knew if I worked hard at it, I would make good money. My job was selling goods to bars, restaurants and hotels. At the time the pub trade was starting to boom in Ireland. As they said at the time, 'A yard of counter was better than a good farm'. As it happened many publicans then had a yard of a counter and a good farm, maybe an undertaking business or a post office. Despite all the perks that were with the pub, it wasn't for everyone. It was a very tempting job for many who were a bit fond of the drink because it was under their nose all the time, seven days and seven nights a week.

Today the scene has changed. Many of these lucrative businesses are struggling. They are being operated by some elderly people who would have long retired if they were in an ordinary job. Sadly, very few of their children are interested in taking over the businesses because of the unsociable hours. For many family owned bars and restaurants nowadays, their greatest challenge may not be in finding staff or customers but trying to cope with the raft of rules and regulations that don't apply in many other European countries or in many parts of the world.

They say that history repeats itself and what goes around comes around. We could see the licence trade going back to the shebeen days. Let's hope that doesn't happen. Let's hope the regulators and lawmakers see the light before it's too late for many prosperous legally run businesses.

Grocery shopping in the '60s was somewhat different to today. At the time it was a necessity, today it's a day out that most people don't like. The choice now would bamboozle Methuselah. The good thing about it now is you have apps to tell you where the goods are displayed, when to use them before and after and what compartment of the refrigerator to store them in. Today the world of retailing is moving on into the future. Where it will end, I don't know.

I see where the giant American supermarket chain Kroger has invented a new way to shop. You can go to your local Kroger supermarket in the US. They have 5,000 of them, pick up your Kroger trolley fitted out with a scanner and pay station. After, simply waltz around the store, pick up the item, scan it on the trolley handle and place it into your trolley. When you have all your shopping done you simply tap your credit card on the handle of the shopping trolley, and you pay for the goods and head out to your car. No queues, no waits. Obviously, that is going to be the future. You won't need tellers, just security at the door so we don't try to cod the shopping trolley operators. No doubt before long someone will 'crack' it.

Back on the floor in Quinnsworth you needed to be a brain surgeon, a magician and a counsellor to be able to explain the working of simple things like Bextartar or Bovril and how to use them. You needed to be a bit of a bluffer as well. The Dubs were great at that. One trader who pretended he knew everything often got himself into a hole. Once a customer asked him what the difference was between plain flour and self-raising flour. His answer was 'there are raisins in the self-raising flour'. Another asked him where she would find dog food. Without lifting his head, he said 'in the pet food section'. I'm not sure if a culchie like me would get away with those answers.

Chapter 11

Dublin in the rare old times

Cities are always attractive places for young people because there are plenty of young people living, working and at college there. I settled in well, out every night on the town, steak, onions and chips in the Pronto Grill in Ranelagh every weekend. Down to Leitrim every Sunday to play a match with my local football club, Gortletteragh, back that evening to Dublin in Mel Sorohan's Volkswagen Beetle. The night life in Ranelagh was electric. No bother getting a flat or a bed for the night if you were stuck. I stayed in a flat in Ashfield Road, around the corner was Mountain View flats on the road to Rathmines.

Many of the houses and flats in this area were regularly robbed. The main items worth robbing were radios or cassettes out of cars. Nobody bothered taking a phone as they wouldn't work once you pulled them off the wall. At that time, like in many other places, there were career criminals who robbed for a living. Shops, cars, houses or anywhere they could get something to sell on.

One Monday morning I was in bed at 11am as Monday was my day off. It was a downstairs flat in Ranelagh. Next thing a gentleman made his way in through the open window in my bedroom with two letters in his hand, presumably a decoy. He was more surprised to see me than I was him as people often locked themselves out of upstairs flats and used to come in via our flat.

There was no aggro – we both said hello and he walked out past my bed, out of the room and out the front door. No kisses blown.

I recognised my visitor at the time as a regular around Ranelagh village. He later went on to become a career criminal by the name of Martin Cahill (The General), who paid the price for criminality with his life.

Molly's Late Night restaurant was a great hangout on Camden Street. The place was frequented by the showbands after the dances around the area. You got special treatment and better food if you were in a showband. I bought myself a fancy black velvet type suit and passed as being in a showband in Molly's. I was favourite there for a couple of years or until Molly's found out I was a liar.

My first car was a Renault Dauphine. It was a great car, when it started. I used to have to park it at the top of the lane, start pushing it, then run after it and jump in it and away she went spluttering and farting. She was fitted with twin exhausts. One was a dummy I fitted myself, so I'd look 'cool'. If you went through a flood of water or it was raining the alternator got wet and she wouldn't start. If you went through a flood, you could be stuck there for the day.

One day I was bringing my father to the pub. A gust of smoke came up from under the bonnet followed by flames. We both jumped out and looked at my prized possession that I paid 40 quid for, up in smoke. My father didn't have much sympathy for me. He looked at me and said, 'We will come back for it and tow it home, it will do as a hen house'.

Chapter 12

The long road to Mayo

The road from Leitrim to Dublin back to Leitrim and onto Mayo had a few twists and turns which I was able to negotiate with a few bumps here and there. I thought Leitrim was the only place in Ireland that was half covered in rushes, bushes, bohalauns and nettles. My first day in Mayo I looked out the window into a swamp filled with all of the above. Every window I looked out was the same. I had bought a house in the middle of a bog where the swans needed waders to negotiate the front garden and the back garden. The driveway into the house was flooded. I bought the house in June not realising when I moved in four months after that I would be surrounded by nature like the Green Party promotes today.

After ten years I was beginning to get a handle on things after spending more outside in the garden and on the driveway than I spent buying the house. I thought 60 acres of this was bad in Leitrim, but it was worse in Mayo because it was staring you in the face day and night.

How did I end up in Mayo? I was regularly asked this question. Well, my late wife Mary had a good pensionable job with Mayo County Council as a librarian. I couldn't convince her to move to Leitrim to the 60 acres, so I was forced to move to a half-acre in Mayo.

From the day I arrived here I became acquainted with a lot of people. Guards from Donegal, publicans from Kerry, doctors from Roscommon, nurses from every county. The town was full of them, both male and female. From day one I had to handle many things from taking 'stick' from fellas who were experts on football and to the men from Mayo who didn't win an All-Ireland in over 70 years. They yearned for the day when they would carry the Sam Maguire shoulder high down every boreen and bog lane in Mayo which hasn't happened yet. I believe the Queen of England, before she died, called all her friends aside to tell them what her greatest regret in life was that she didn't live to see Mayo win the All-Ireland. There is no truth in the rumour that Prince Charles, now King Charles, replied, 'Let's see how many they win in my term of office, I'll update you when I meet you on the other side'. Is he being optimistic or sarcastic?

Mayo has always been the hot bed of politics. There have been great stories told down the years, some of which are unrepeatable. Shortly after I moved here there was a gentleman who was from the next parish to America who was Chairman of Mayo County Council. At one special meeting attended by all the councillors and county executives the plan was to strike a rate that farmers, businesses and households would pay on their property. They had to agree on the rate at the meeting. If not, the county manager would abolish the council and take matters into his own hands.

As things turned out they couldn't agree, which is unusual in politics. When this happened the county manager said, 'in that case you're abolished'. The chairman, having misread the manager, jumped to his feet and shouted at the manager, 'and you are a bollocks as well'. It wasn't the first or last time derogatory words were thrown at members of the council. Mayo was noted for it for a few decades.

Politics is a funny game. Not funny 'haha' but funny 'peculiar'. There are many funny decisions made. That can happen in any job or any walk of life. The media always seemed to be obsessed with reporting on the happenings at council meetings and national politics. Our lives were taken over every night watching what happened in the Dáil, the Seanad or in the local courts. We all love to see what the criminals are up to and who is before the count for after hours. They usually target a certain business for selling drink to underage children. Seldom will you see a multinational supermarket prosecuted for selling drink to underage children. It's obvious nowadays that's where young people get the drink, either there or at home.

I didn't drink until I was 19. There was nothing unusual about that in those days. There are still a lot of 19-year olds who are not drinking. Drink has been our greatest pastime and obsession whether talking about it or thinking about it. The only reason this is the case is because we all remember our forefathers talking about prohibition in America. We all read about the unfortunate poteen maker in Connemara being rounded by the gardaí and his top quality 'wash' being dumped out of the barrels into the nearby drain. This created the fight back. I believe that's how we got the name 'The Fighting Irish'. The poteen was a very potent liquor. It was easy to make if you knew how. I knew families who made a lucrative living out of it. I know one family who paid for at least one son to go to college and become a priest. The priest was often referred to as 'The Poteen Priest'.

He was a pioneer who told us all how we would burn in the fires of hell if we neglected the family by overindulging in drink. It was even said he used to go down to the pub, wait outside the door at closing time to try and get some of the drunkards on the way out to kneel down and he would give them the pledge. The poteen criminals are getting fewer. Another breed of more ruthless criminals has come along where nobody is interested in stopping their illicit sales of anything illegal.

Chapter 13

Slaving for a living on the highways and byways

My first job in Mayo was as a traveller or a travelling salesman, calling to bars and restaurants replacing glasses, cups and saucers the customers had stolen or broken the weeks before. Everyone with a handbag would arrive home with an ashtray or a fancy wine glass. Other times you were forced into thievery when the guards raided the pub and you had to run out the back door with the pint you had only taken one mouthful from.

The main duty of every garda in most towns was to clear the pubs. It didn't always work because the guard could run them out the front door and they ran in the back door. They could end up inside for two or three hours as the guard might be outside the front door to 'snare' them again. Today there is no need to raid most pubs as many drinkers are gone before closing time.

The pub scene took off in the early '70s. New bars opened up; old bars were renovated. Singing lounges were built in the middle of nowhere. Every weekend and sometimes during the week, big bands played everywhere. There were over 1,000 bands in Ireland as well as local groups who were popular in their own area. Yankees came back from America to open ballrooms and by the '70s the country was alive with entertainment. From Belmullet to Bundoran, from Rooskey to Roscrea, there was a ballroom everywhere and a pub on every crossroads with big bands playing there.

The '70s and '80s are often referred to as 'the bad old days in Ireland'. That was a myth. At the time the pubs were packed nearly every night. Half of the country was drawing the dole. A lot of them had a job on the side. The revenue commissioners were happy if you were in business, and you paid them something. The government owed less than a billion pounds. There was money there to fill potholes in roads and give a good service in every hospital in the land.

Today the taxmen have upped their skills at revenue collection. We have the best revenue collection system in Europe. They come here to see how we do it. We don't owe €1 billion anymore. We owe about €301 billion and it's rising. We have a slight problem with looking after our people in hospitals or giving any type of up to date service. Sadly, the people who get most of the stick for cockups nowadays are the people at the coalface instead of looking into systems and the people who run the systems. Despite all our ups and downs, we are still classed as one of the wealthiest countries in the world.

I never got too bogged down in politics even though I have a good few friends in politics. I don't envy their jobs. It's not a nine to five job and the hours can be very unsociable. Over the years I was approached a number of times to see if I would run for election. It wasn't my scene. Anyway, I was doing more hours than most politicians sometimes for less money. I'm not sure why people had an interest in me running for election. Maybe they could get nobody else.

My response was always the same: 'I'd love to go for election, but I have one great fear, the fear I would get elected and then regret it'. That was the end of that.

In business over the years I dealt with county councillors, TDs, senators and ministers who at some stage owned pubs or restaurants. They were, as a rule, good contacts to have. They could put in a word for you here and there where a friend of theirs was opening a pub somewhere.

Business nowadays is more about social media, apps, online selling and websites. Before that it was about getting out and about making contacts, giving a good service and being honest. Once you picked up a good customer and looked after them, they stayed with you. The new world of selling is more about technology to do things more simply. Despite that, old technology is still important to keep in the agenda.

We all have our heroes and icons in life. We like to imitate them. These may be people who made it in sport, business or just from being nice people. Many people in business can remember the people who forgot to pay you for goods they supplied. Others you can remember for the 'turn' they did for you.

Selling goods on the road can be a challenge anywhere because chances are you will have four or five more operators selling the same goods you are, and you have to compete. Getting a job with a company where the products they had sold themselves was every salesperson's dream. It was a job for life which wasn't everyone's cup of tea. Oftentimes the challenges weren't there. You could have a good lifestyle, play golf and bring your customers to the races.

Most of that scene is gone with the wind because everything now in big business is about the 'bottom line' profit. The war in Ukraine has proved that oil companies and energy suppliers are inflating prices to take advantage of the situation just to boost profits. If you have shares in any of these companies, you may be on a killing because their share prices and dividends are rising. President Biden had told these companies not to be exploiting the situation by rising prices for oil and gas that cost no more to produce today than they did three years ago.

God help the poor American motorists; they are now paying $3.60 a gallon for gasoline while us rich Irish pay nearly €10 per gallon. Despite that it is some consolation we are only paying €10 a gallon for diesel as we are now paying up to €40 a gallon for our favourite stout or lager, €2,200 a kilo for caviar and €8,200 a kilo for truffles which are now part of my daily diet. Amazingly you can still buy a kilo of Irish potatoes for less than 60c and you won't get drunk on them provided you don't try to make poteen out of them.

Chapter 14

The watchtower that became a lighthouse

After I arrived in Castlebar I bought a house two miles outside the town in the middle of, you guessed it, a swamp. It was surrounded by bog. The front garden was full of water, weeds and anything useless that grows in a swamp. I thought I had left all that behind me in Leitrim. This was the biggest battle I had on my hands, trying to get water out of cutaway bogs in my front garden with drains that were overgrown with weeds, bog, soil and water that was going nowhere.

I got expert advice on how to handle a situation like this from people who knew what to do but didn't know how to do it. I knew it would be costly to fill the swamp and there was still no guarantee I would have a good garden to grow anything except more weeds and bauhalans, which are a curse to get rid of. The only way you can get rid of them is to buy a dozen pigs and they would root up the roots and eat them. The other problem was you can be prosecuted for allowing bauhalans to grow on your land because the flowers on them are poisonous. Problem was most roadsides around the west are filled with them on the grass margins and the seeds blow into the adjoining fields and take root. This would have been another battle I would have to sort.

The fact was I couldn't get the water to go anywhere unless I dug a six-foot drain to the nearest river. I was snookered. My only option if I couldn't get rid of the water and weeds was to clean it and make a lake out of it, which I did. I started rearing goldfish, frogs and feeding the mink that came around to eat the fish. As a warning to these thieving bastards, I built a watchtower with a light and foghorn in it.

More trouble coming. I was approached one day by a member of the local council who wanted to know what the contraption in the middle of the lake was. I told him it was a watchtower. He asked me had I planning for my watchtower. I told him I didn't have planning as I thought I didn't need it. He told me you need planning permission for a watchtower, but you don't need planning permission for a lighthouse. I thought for a minute and realised my watchtower was surrounded by water; it was, in effect, a lighthouse I built, not a watchtower. Problem solved.

It's better having this type of activity in my garden than the council prosecuting me for growing bauhalans that could poison the country and me.

The lighthouse and the lake are there so I have no grass to cut, no fish to feed because the mink took the lot of them. The frogs, bees and birds are making a home inside the watchtower, sorry, lighthouse, and a family of wild ducks come every year to visit and rear their family. The swallows have a permanent holiday home in the rafters of the lighthouse. So, we are all happy, except the mink who has no fish to eat. No doubt they will change their menu to a few laying hens who they can easily catch off guard.

I had planned to shoot some of the mink who killed my goldfish with my legally held shotgun. I was told you cannot shoot mink or foxes, even if they are looking over the wall at me every night hoping I'll move away so they can capture some of my fish or hens.

Chapter 15

My problem with weight, drink, doctors and dieticians

From when I reached the use of reason, I had a major problem with drink. It was the price of it. I resented the government taking €50 out of every €100 I drank. They should have paid me €50 for every time I woke up with a pain in my head, a sick stomach and bulging eyes. I promised myself several times that I wasn't going to drink any more … Or drink any less for that part.

We all go off the drink now and again to give the mind and body a break. I usually did it for the first two days of Lent and then bang, you meet someone who is having a birthday party and I was gone again back to my wayward ways. I stopped promising myself I was going to give up the cursed thing because I always told lies to myself and broke every promise. Most people in life have battles with themselves and others. The battle with yourself is often the hardest battle to win.

My fondness of the good things in life was the main reason I was overweight. Again, it was one of those things I battled with for most of my natural life. I was always told by dietitians and doctors and other concerned people that I should lose weight. My doctor never let me alone. So, I decided I would go on a diet.

I arrived in the surgery, stripped down to the bare essentials. First thing he said, 'You're carrying a bit of weight'. I never heard of many people who were told they needed to put on weight.

Before he threw me up on the scales he asked me, 'What weight do you reckon you are?' I said probably 18.5 stone of prime Irish meat. He threw me up on the scales that you would break your back trying to look over my belly to see the numbers going like a

Ferrari car from 0 to 100 in two seconds. He asked me what was
the heaviest I was in the past few years. I was over 20 stone once.
He asked me what the lightest I was. I said 7lb and 10oz. He had a
battle on his hands to get me back to that. He told me the best approach was to cut out white bread and anything with sugar in it,
which is almost everything – chocolate, bananas, grapes. Eat plenty
of roughage, porridge, better known as stirabout. No fancy drinks
or stuff that gives you indigestion.

Amazingly all the stuff he recommended was stuff that made
you fart. Drinking of alcohol was out. Like every doctor who asks
you how many units of alcohol you drink in the week, you tell him
you drink 20 units. I'm not sure if a unit is a glass, a pint or a gallon.
If you drink 20 units, he will tell you to cut it down to ten units. If
you tell him you drink four units, he tells you to cut it down to two
units.

If you smoke, you're in the manure business and he tells you
'Give up the fags or they will kill ya'. If you get a cough or a sore
throat and you to go the doctor, the first thing he will ask is, 'Do
you smoke?' 'No, I haven't smoked in 30 years.' He then tells you,
'That's the cause of your cough and your sore throat'. If I followed
all the advice and instruction I would have ended up like a Tibetan
monk or a nun in the Poor Clare Order not being allowed to open
my mouth to eat or drink or talk.

I still made it until now to tell my story. As for professional advice from me … 'Live for today because tomorrow you shall diet'.

Chapter 16

How it's better to be poor than rich

During my life people often told me I should have become a stunt driver because I had so many mishaps. I had, like everyone, a few ups and downs and some near misses in life. From a young age I was prone to accidents, like most people who are reared on a farm are. I was always seeking adventure. The first blow I got was when I was seven and I fell out of a tree in the grounds of Lough Rynn Castle and broke an arm. A few years later I fell off a building and broke a leg.

As I moved into later life I got cancer, prostate problems, heart problems and the usual cholesterol, high blood pressure and diabetes. If you don't have one or all of these nowadays, there is something wrong with you.

I thought most of my troubles were over until I got run over by a squad car and was out of work for months.

In 2006 I was holidaying in Spain. At a bullfight in the town of Ronda I was chased down the main street by a raging bull that got loose out of his compound. Obviously, he was looking for a fight. He didn't know he picked on the wrong fella to have a fight with. I ran as fast as I could before I was hauled over a wall by onlookers.

I was at the stage where I was living in a world where I had the view that it wasn't safe to be alive. I didn't give up and still haven't. I have put all of these behind me and moved on with a few bumps and bruises to show.

I have always read about unfortunate people in life, like one Adolphe Sax. He was said to be one of the most unfortunate people in the world. During his early life, at two years of age, he split his head with a falling brick. He went on to poison himself three times by drinking sulphuric acid, thinking it was milk. He later swallowed a needle and he fell face down onto a sizzling skillet. He drank a glass of varnish his father used in his furniture workshop.

It didn't stop young Sax achieving his ambitions in life. He went on to invent the saxophone. Since then I have often been told that I should have invented the bouncy castle or tree swings. It's not too late yet.

I have since been christened all sorts of names like Houdini and some less charming names.

When, in later life, I was diagnosed with throat cancer, my consultant in Galway was more concerned about me than I was about me. After 20 sessions of radiotherapy, I got the all clear.

On one of my visits to my consultant in University Hospital, Galway we debated Mayo football, Leitrim football and many other serious issues in life, more important than mine. On one visit she asked me how I was feeling and had I any issues. The only issue I told her I had was I used to be able to sing like Johnny Cash and with my new change of vocal cords I could no longer sing like Cash. Quick off the mark she said, 'You will probably be singing like Ronnie Drew from now on'.

Then came the pandemic and I had to practice my singing to the wall or in the bath. The pubs were closed so the music died. Thankfully for all our sanity's sake it has returned with a lot of new outfits on the road playing to bigger crowds. One group who played for me in the pub before the pandemic have hit the big time since.

The Mary Wallopers took to the big road after Covid. They are now drawing thousands of fans on their Irish, English and American tours. That's why my view is you're better off to be born with talent where you have the get up and go to better yourself rather than being born rich with a silver spoon in your mouth where you never need to work. Eventually the silver spoon may rust. The money may run out and you could be back to owning very little. That doesn't matter once you're happy. My philosophy is, there is no shame in being poor, it's just the inconvenience of it. I know the comments I get when I mention that to people who are 'tight' with the money and don't like spending. My time working in Africa with Niall Mellon showed me how irrelevant money can be if you're not treated with respect at home.

My mother used to say about so and so down the road that he hadn't a dog's life in his household because of the way he was treated. The cat, the dog, the pony or the hamster are sometimes better looked after than humans. So, thank your lucky stars you have a roof over your head and a bed to sleep in and a hamster and a dog to bring you for long walks in the country.

Chapter 17

What we should thank the Brits for

Many people in republican circles may not agree with me but the British gave the world a lot of infrastructure that made life simpler for everyone. I wonder if they didn't take over half the world, would we in the west have all we do today? Maybe yes, maybe no. We could say the Spanish, the Portuguese, the Romans and even the Russians left their mark.

It's understandable that when these empires took over places, their plan was to own them forever.

The best approach then was to nourish, look after and develop them. This was often done at a huge cost to peoples' lives and integrity. Nobody likes to be bossed nowadays, nobody likes to be told what to do even though we are being told everyday what we must do and how we do it. You may not be told personally but it is usually spelled out in letters in brown envelopes with windows in them.

The west and midlands probably gained more from British technology in the past. Many British lords took over large swipes of land and built mansions like today's mansions. They could have immunity and security by living at the other end of the country, by changing their name to Lord so and so instead of Mr so and so. Amazingly all these landlords were men. Leitrim gained a lot from British technology and knowhow as indeed Mayo and Galway did where there were many stately houses and castles, many of which are now being operated as top-class hotels.

The greatest lasting infrastructures they left were the canals they built and the railroads they built and maintained. You could say they built these infrastructures for themselves. Maybe so but the people of Ireland did have access to them to transport goods and enjoy our waterways which are probably the best in the world, when they don't flood half the country. Sadly, many of these great facilities were abandoned when the British left this part of Ireland.

Many of the railway stations were closed down and the imposing buildings left to rot. The tracks were pulled up and sold off for a pittance to farmers to build hay sheds. The sleepers were dumped in CIE yards and compounds across the country. The canals which they built from the centre of Dublin through five counties ended up in the Shannon at Tarmonbarry. The Shannon continued on into Northern Ireland through a maze of lakes, rivers and more canals.

Today the canal from Dublin to the Shannon is overgrown in most places even though these types of facilities are being opened and promoted across the world. A simple solution to solve Dublin's water shortage, even though they are surrounded by water, would be to throw a four or five foot pipe into the canal from Tarmonbarry to Dublin and ship any amount needed to help the thirsty Dubliners. It could be undertaken in a short time instead of digging drains for underground pipes from Tipperary at a cost of €3 billion which may end up at €10 billion if things go well.

Sadly, too many of the old, well-built country houses which the British built were either burned down or left to fall just because a ruthless British landlord owned them. We should have had the cop on to realise that when these people died or left the country, they couldn't bring these assets with them.

Today the Shannon is one of the greatest waterways in Europe. It creates thousands of jobs even though it flooded our land in Leitrim every time we had a bad season of rain. I think I'll blame the Brits for this because they should have come back and drained it again. It's been over 100 years since it was last drained. We have to blame them for something. If we don't blame them, we blame the other villain that destroys all our lives that we can never stop talking about – the weather. Where would we be without the rain? We would have no crops, no wheat, barley, oats, garlic or onions. We would be depending on the Chinese and the Spanish and the French to supply us with all these goods for our French onion soup.

Imagine if we had no rain and we had the weather like they have in the Sahara or if we were like Spain, our economy would be a freefall with half of our retail shops out of business. No shops selling wellingtons, umbrellas, caps, raingear, mops or mop buckets, flood barriers, water gullies or drainpipes. We wouldn't be able to watch Irish TV and look at half the midlands covered in water and the people of Dublin crying crocodile tears for the poor bastards who have to use a boat to get into their homes. Events like these get people talking about the weather, not about how we could handle flooding by draining our rivers and canals. Sorry, that's not allowed anymore because frogs, porcupines, bats, beetles and badgers (seem to) have a better place in society than humans. That's another form of racism.

We should be all classed as equals. If the fish can swim in the sea, I should have that right too. If the frogs, beetles, bats or pine martens can come into my house when I leave the door open and kill my pet budgie, I should be allowed to visit and invade their habitat and at the same time show respect to them if they show respect to my budgie.

My favourite little creature, or my alarm clock every morning growing up, was the corncrake. Sadly, the batteries ran out and today it is very unusual to see or hear a corncrake. We could have and should have. We had all the evidence that modern farming and the use of mechanical mowers were going to destroy their habitat and way of life. The farmers' livelihoods are built around tillage and cutting grass so you cannot blame them.

Maybe the Greens could have come up with a plan to find a safe haven for the corncrakes.

When I was growing up on a small farm in Leitrim, it was an era in Ireland where we were nearly self-sufficient. We didn't depend on many others to feed or cloth us. We grew our own fruit and vegetables. We produced our own meat. The bed we slept in had an Odearest mattress, constellation sheets and Foxford blankets, all made in Ireland. The six most popular yokes around the house were made in China. The hot water bottles, the holy water bottles, the clothes pegs, the clothesline, the China mugs and the China teapots were all part of the family essentials. Most of these have been diluted. The only two that have stuck the pace of time are the clothes pegs and the clothesline. Most of the hot water bottles are buried in the bottom of wardrobes or under the bed. As for the holy water bottles or the holy water fonts – they have dried out.

The China tea sets are a decoration in the new modern Ikea kitchen units. The China mugs are getting fewer, they have been replaced by clumsier, pottery mugs which are similar to the Arklow pottery mugs of the '40s or the '50s.

We have a lot to thank the Chinese for and we have a lot to thank ourselves for. Our forefathers knew what the art of survival was about. They could survive and make allowances for shortages and rationing unlike today, where the world can nearly come to a standstill if there is an energy shortage or a shortage of chips to run cars and computers. Health wise we are faring worse than the people of other eras. If the Chinese get a cough, we get Covid. When our cough goes it gets back to China, they get Covid.

Are they just being cagey? Check out to see how much the world depends on them when they close up one or two cities that produce a lot of goods for the west. Are they holding back supplies of goods until prices go up? Anything is possible.

These are some of the oldest tricks in the business book. Create a shortage and everyone wants to fill their houses with the stuff. One only has to look at the Marmite scare a few years ago. There was a scarcity of the stuff and everyone wanted it, even the people who never tasted Marmite in their life or knew what it was for.

As for the scarcity of toilet paper … It's the best product in the world to create a scarcity of because it's a product we cannot live or operate without. Despite the fact it was scarce during Covid, you could buy it in supermarkets, pharmacies, hardware shops, garden centres or in any outlet or car boot sale where a bit of extra space can be found to display it. None of us want to go back to the past and start using the natural toilet paper many of our ancestors were forced to use. It's not recommended. It might not be a runner because very few people buy their daily newspaper anymore. Maybe with new technology and apps we will see the day when toilet paper will be no more. I'm sure there are people out there working on that. Will someone let me know when they crack it as I want to do my part in protecting the environment and saving the ozone layer.

The Railway Times

The Brits were the ones who put them there
Those naughty boys, they should never have been here
They built the railroads to every town
To last forever, in the worst of times.

The greatest way to travel around
It cost so little, maybe half a crown
From Dromad to Dublin, home and back
It rattled and roared, along the track.

Through bogs and fields and the countryside
You see cows grazing between bushes and wheat
The fertile planes around midland towns
Were the envy of us all from barren ground.

They're gone from many a country town
No replacement or thought for those left around
Who cares that progress is in a sorry state
By the lack of brains, from Ireland's greats

– *Oliver Kelleher* (2008)

Chapter 18

Chips and controversy

My early life in Dublin was all about social media, socialising and reading papers. Every night after a session in The Chariot Inn or Russell's Pub in Ranelagh, we would head for the best place in town for chips. They were in abundant supply.

Since then, we have had a major shortage of 'chips'. It's so bad you can't make a car or drive a car now without chips. You can't drive a tractor or a computer without chips. I never thought I'd see the day. Never did I think we would see social media become a yoke you use on your phone or computer to talk to or talk about everyone. I never thought that most of the pubs in Ireland would stop selling drink so we could all become pioneers and the health authorities would solve the great Irish drinking culture where we got the name of being the best drinkers, revellers and fighters in the world. That was and is a myth because other countries have a much better record than us.

These places are often classed as more civilised drinkers because they drink cheap off-licence beers, wines and spirits from the many foreign supermarkets and off-licences, where you can become an alcoholic on less than a tenner on the cheap foreign beer everyone writes and talks about.

Modern technology, social media and apps have given us all an endless supply of information. This information is not very well regulated simply because it is owned and operated by big businesses who in the modern world can write their own rules. This can be an advantage to some and a disadvantage to others. Ask Donald Trump about his dealings with Twitter when they banned him from their platform. I saw that happen once where a fella was banned from a pub. He went back six months later and bought the pub. It was an expensive way of getting an apology. It didn't work like that for Donald Trump so he set up his own social media company that promises to tell the truth, 'no porkies'. I wish him luck.

Despite his insistence on telling the truth, nearly all of the time or some of the time, he was once asked 'Did you ever tell a lie?' His response was 'I only tell a lie when I have to'. Are you one of those people? I think we all are at some time or another. I know one thing for certain – when he returns home from the pub half 'scuttered' after 12 pints and the wife asks him how many pints he had. Six was always the answer. A lie was the appropriate answer there.

Like business, religion can be a ruthless business too. Trying to defend oneself and the system from attack can be a challenge. Sometimes no matter what you do, you can be wrong in the eyes of many. When priests and bishops stepped out of line in the past, they and the church they represented were dragged over the coals. This was particularly evident with men in the Catholic Church. Nuns as a rule didn't get the same lash back. These things only seemed to have happened within the Catholic Church. Maybe it happened in the Church of Ireland but we weren't aware of it.

Growing up I never knew much about our protestant neighbours. Did they go to Mass? Did they have a God like we have? Did they go to confessions? Had they a hell hole like we had where you were likely to meet every conman or murderer that ever inhabited the world if you were unlucky?

In my early days we were all controlled with fear. If you do that, you'll get this at school. You dare not use the F word or any letter or word that upset people. Religion played a big part in our lives and the governments let them look after many issues that had no bearing on religion.

The church was a powerful force and we all respected their authority and the service they provided to families, the sick and old which they still do to this day. They may have been a bit too one sided in many people's minds. As young people became more up to date with the world around them, they started to question things. Some clergy men and women did the same and many of them left their vocation behind.

Bishop Éamonn Casey was a shining light in the Catholic Church at organising any event. He was crucified before he died. I attended his funeral in March 2017 at the Cathedral in Galway.

Like all of us when we die, they will probably say nice things about us and rightly so. At the time I was a columnist with the *Western People* so I felt in my heart I should give my opinions on the events on the day of Bishop Casey's burial.

Chapter 19

Bishop Casey

Last month I attended the Funeral Mass for the late Bishop Éamonn Casey. During the 90-minute service my thoughts were miles away from the lessons my mother taught me on how and what to do when you go to Church. The idea of ensuring I pray enough to save my soul didn't play much part in my mind in the Cathedral in Galway. I was more tuned into the problems the Catholic Church has and had over the past 30 years. My own salvation came somewhere down the line. As I wondered, having listened to and watched 40 priests and some six bishops outline the career of Bishop Casey, I felt there isn't much difference between politics and religion. For years Bishop Casey was ostracised by his own flock. Having an affair with a female was – and still is – a taboo subject in the Catholic Church. Having a sexual relationship with a woman and a sibling born out of that relationship is probably the worst thing that can happen in the Catholic Church.

The Church often comes across as a caring organisation and we still have a lot of very caring people within the Catholic Church. To most people Bishop Casey gave a lot to society among the Irish in the UK where he worked hard to promote Irish values and help people who were less fortunate. Unlike politicians or the Church, he put a roof over the heads of many Irish people in England in the '60s when he organised lending institutions to lend to them to buy houses at a time when we couldn't even offer them work here in Ireland. His ability to organise people was akin to some of the great religious leaders from around the world and particularly here in Mayo. The clerics at his Funeral Mass outlined the contribution Bishop Casey made to society and the people he represented. They outlined his life and times, his ups and downs and the mistakes he made in life which he was forced to apologise for many, many times.

All these apologies did little to reinstate the Catholic Church to what it had been in the years previous. The apologies drove a wedge between the Bishop and Annie Murphy and his son. Apologising for something that two people did should not have to happen. Nobody died and the events that took place were between two consenting adults.

The sermons on the day made me think of how so often we are away from reality. 'He who doesn't have a sin among them cast the first stone' seemed somewhat hypocritical because there were many stones fired in his time of 'trouble'. He was ostracised, not allowed to say Mass or do his priestly duties when and where he chose. All the talent and work he had shown and the contribution to society was forgotten. The attitude was: we don't want him in our organisation because he speaks his mind and does things in life that good Catholics are not allowed to do or say.

That's why during the service I became somewhat disillusioned when I realised there isn't much difference between politics and religion. They have more or less the same rules and principles. Nobody was going to cast the last stone when someone is dead and cannot speak their mind. There is a change of heart and all the good things in life that people did come flooding back the day you are being buried. The Church uses this approach in many walks of life whether the people deserve to be recognised or not.

Recently I listened to a sermon given by a clergyman from the pulpit at the burial of a serial criminal who had murdered people. 'He was a family man who was cherished by all his family. He left a partner and two young children who would no longer have the security of both parents.' When this person was alive the Church or State had no views or comments to make on his wayward and brutal ways of life when he caused grief.

That's why I say that religion and some people are hypocrites when it suits. We see the same in politics where politicians will have one view today and another view tomorrow depending on what suits them. How does it affect us? For most, including myself, it doesn't bother me one way or the other because I know it won't change. We are all liars at times. There are different types of lies. One is a 'bare faced' lie which is the most popular. These are lies where everyone knows they are liars, and the liar refuses to accept the majority view. The other is an existing lie. This is where someone adds a 'bit' to a story to ensure people are tuned into what you are saying or telling them. This is more often practiced by comedians. I think it was Spike Milligan who said, 'An exciting lie sounds better than a boring truth'.

When Bishop Casey passed away it was the end of an era for the Catholic Church. His life and times created an era of controversy and questions as to what was happening within the Church. The cover ups and the dictatorial attitude as to how people should behave. Times have changed. What shocked society in the past is now a one-day wonder. Maybe the Church should change to reflect the world of equality for men and women priests. Maybe they should tell things as they are, not as they like to be told. Maybe the people who have a voice, whether you agree with them or not, should be heard. It's not the way religion or politics works. It's a hypocritical trade to be in. The important thing for those engaged in it is they should know how to handle it. With the right training and plenty of grinds it becomes simple. Whether they are right or wrong, it may not matter because people like the late Bishop Éamonn will always do things their own way without ever injuring anyone. They are remembered affectionately as caring people who don't always play by the rules who sinners love to 'fire' stones at.

As I moved away from the crypt at the Cathedral in Galway where the remains of Ireland's best-known cleric were interred, I found a pen and copied down that line, 'He who has no sin let him cast the first stone'. I wondered would we hold another inquiry as to how that phrase should work in practice because the stones nowadays never seem to stop 'flying' because a lot of people think they are always right.

Chapter 20

Living your dreams and being happy

People everywhere go through life living their dreams. These dreams can be varied, controversial, dangerous and exciting. Some have dreams and aspirations to become doctors, to help save the world. Others aspire to be successful athletes and win awards because they are the best in their field.

My dreams were about being happy in life, getting a job that I liked and working with people I liked. Things worked out pretty well for me in achieving that. Obviously if you could be rewarded financially for your efforts, that was a bonus. Those times money was the least important until you ran out of money and then it became the most important part of life. That time you had neighbours in the area who would do a day or two of work for us and they wouldn't expect to get paid, but you gave them two days in return, no money changed hands. The taxman was not involved, no stamps, PRSI or deductions.

A neighbour of mine went to England in the '60s. He got a job with a subbie in London. He joined a crew of 20 more digging trenches for water pipes. They were going well but there was no sign of any money or wages coming. After three months the subbie called them into the office he had, a battered 40-foot container which doubled up as the canteen as well. He had an issue, not a problem. He said, 'I'm afraid I don't have any money to pay you for the past three months'. Obviously, there were long faces all around until one buck piped up and said, 'Ah not to worry, sure it was good to get the work' and they all moved on to work directly for McAlpine.

Being happy at what you do is one thing but staying happy is another. Having a positive approach is a good tonic. We all can get down. It's all part of life. The most important thing is not to get 'down and out'. I don't know where that phrase came from, but I do remember people when I was young who were down and out. The phrase and the people never leaves my mind. These were the people who threw in the towel. They might have lost their job, had no job, went on the drink or hit hard times which a lot of people did during the hard times of the past when there were no dole, handouts or fuel allowances. Most of these down and outs found it difficult to shake off the 'out' bit.

The same thing is happening today. Many people lose their homes because they cannot pay the mortgage. Obviously, this will have a major effect on their way of life and causes them and their family to be down. When your home is repossessed that's the sad part because you then become 'down and out'. We don't make that reference to people anymore and rightly so because it is a stigma that is hard to shake off.

I used to hear comments made about people who hit hard times and couldn't cope. He was a 'down and out' in London once, but he is 'back on track'. When I spoke to those people, they often felt proud of the fact they were down and outs but pulled themselves together and did well in life. They were the lucky ones. For some, life, times and events can be cruel where you end up in a rut that's hard to dig yourself out of.

I don't like seeing people in these situations, especially someone I know who went off the rails, hit hard times, had a run in with the family and moved out of home. I often can spot these types of people when I see them. Maybe it's because I look out for them. They can have a huge impact on your life and ways of thinking.

During one of the Covid-19 lockdowns, when I was a columnist with the *Western People*, I came across one of these unfortunate people walking the streets of Castlebar carrying his home in three carrier bags. I wanted to tell the world what was happening around us. The things we can do something about. The things that can be difficult to do something about and the things we can do very little about. This was the column I wrote at the time, and I think it tells its own story.

Chapter 21

Carrying his home in three carrier bags

A nother lockdown is happening. This one isn't as bad as the last one because we may be used to them every few weeks. For many it's anything but pleasant. Trying to cope in a world where the only way you get any attention is if you are diagnosed with the virus. Nothing else seems to matter too much.

On the first day of the latest lockdown I moved a bit around Castlebar town. Nobody was saying too much about anything. We have said it all before. We heard it all before. When the streets are quiet you may take more notice of what's happening or what's not happening. I can usually judge people by their appearance or the way they walk or how they are behaving. As I stood on the footpath, I couldn't help noticing a young man I felt wasn't in a happy mood. He seemed lost as he walked slowly up the Main Street. I followed him and we spoke at the junction at the top of the town.

I put the conversation to him. I asked him where he was from. I told him my name and he told me his name. He was lost in this big, crazy world. He was carrying his home in three carrier bags. I asked him if he had a bed for the night. He hadn't. He had to move out of the apartment he had in Castlebar. 'Peter' (not his real name) was on his way to the garda station to try and arrange to see a social worker who might be able to help him. The gardaí are often put in an awkward spot in these types of situations that they are not trained to handle.

Peter seemed to have found himself in this predicament in the last few weeks. He had some sort of falling out with his family in the previous weeks. I asked him for his phone number. He told me his phone was dead. I offered to give him my number and I offered to buy him a meal. There was no place open and if there was, we would have to eat outside. He didn't know what he wanted or where he wanted to go. Peter is one of the thousands of people in

Ireland right now who don't know where they are going and nobody is there to advise them of the best path because everyone is tied up looking at just one health issue that has preoccupied our minds for the past eight months. The balance is wrong. We may be creating the greatest mental health issue this country has ever seen. We may be in the process of creating the greatest homeless issues this country has ever seen. Our young people have a huge burden put on their shoulders. Parents and guardians have huge pressures piled on them trying to keep a handle on their finances, their families and many more who depend on them.

I don't know where Peter is today but I felt and still feel sorry for him and all the other people who are in the same situation with no place to call home and no light at the end of the tunnel. We have no time to help people who are in this situation. Any little help would make a huge difference instead of waiting for things to fester and get out of control.

Peter isn't an asylum seeker who had to flee from Syria or some other terrible spot. He is one of our own from twelve miles down the road from Castlebar. Fifty years ago, he would have a good chance of getting a place to stay from some neighbour or friend. There would be some place he could go to for a cup of coffee and a chat with people. In the times we live in now that may not be an option because almost everywhere that matters is in lockdown. The experts may look at the benefits of lockdown which the World Health Organisation suggests as a last resort. Is that the stage we are at? It seems to be. The last resort may end up much worse than the first resort for people trying to survive in a world that doesn't care.

Sadly, Peter is another one of those people displaced in a crazy world that's obsessed with a virus we know little or nothing about. On the day I met Peter he was wandering the streets aimlessly carrying his home in three carrier bags. That's not what we came into this world to do. It was a sad scene I will remember for a long time because no one wants to be in it.

Chapter 22

Moving to Mayo and writing for the papers

Castlebar has been home to me for nearly five decades. After the wedding celebrations Mary and myself headed to New York on the honeymoon. First day in New York at the St Patrick's Day parade the streets were lined with everyone and anyone from every county in Ireland, every yankie who wanted to be Irish on the day, every Irish person in New York and from many more countries.

Within one hour I met a neighbour who had emigrated to America a few years previous. She congratulated me on getting married two days before. I said it didn't take you long to find out we got married, she said her mother wrote to her two weeks ago and said I was getting married and we were going to New York and to keep an eye out for us.

On an evening tour of Castlebar, like many Irish towns, I realised there were three undertakers. One buried the Fianna Fáilers, one buried the Fine Gaelers and the other buried the Protestants. I was never aware of these happenings in Leitrim. The most important thing for us wasn't who buried you, provided you weren't left overground regardless of what colour, creed or religion you were.

At that time the country was inhabited by Fianna Fáilers, Fine Gaelers, Protestants and Catholics with a few ludermauns, amadauns, lugs, haverals and head cases thrown in to balance the equation. Nobody cared which group you were, provided you didn't upset the 'applecart'.

Life was simple if you wanted to keep it simple. If you got involved in politics or religious debates you could get clobbered in a pub, outside the church or at a football match. It was survival of the fittest if and when it came to blows. I never got involved. I was part of the peaceful, more serene section of society who felt it was better to say nothing and keep saying it. At times it was hard to keep my trap shut but I felt it paid off in the end. I had learned my lesson from watching cattle jobbers at the fair in Mohill fighting over a few bob and then they went drinking after to celebrate.

Myself and Mary made Castlebar our home where our four children were born and reared. Two of them still live in Castlebar, Sinead and Sharon with a daughter Helen in Australia and my son Ronan in Dublin. Most of my life in Mayo I spent working as a commercial traveller selling hygiene and catering equipment to pubs, restaurants, hotels and businesses in the west and midlands.

It was an exciting time over the years because of the lifestyle people had. The pub was the place to meet before a football match, after Mass on a Sunday and after confessions on a Saturday. Wheeling and dealing was done at the fair in Castlebar and Belmullet. There was a hooley when the immigrants returned at Christmas and Easter.

Lifestyles changed with the smoking ban. Then there were drink driving laws and a raft of new regulations that hit the licenced trade more than any other trades. The plan was to make us a drink free nation. It wasn't going to happen because off-licences opened up on every street corner.

For over seven years I wrote an opinion column in *The Connaught Telegraph* and the *Western People* and other publications. During that time, I was regularly asked, 'Why don't you write a book?' Eventually, when I decided to take the plunge and I told people 'I'm thinking of writing a book', they sort of questioned my ability to write a book. 'Ah sure you wouldn't have the time to write a book, you're so busy'.

Contemplating writing a book for me was like a build-up of anger in me. You have to get it out, you want to tell people all the things that upset you. The things you enjoy. The people who upset you. The people you enjoy being around. I presume everyone is like that, but they may not think about it or care too much about it.

I often wondered if John McGahern felt the same when he was sitting in the sitting room of his home outside Mohill looking out the window at the lake in front of the house, looking for new ideas for his books or poems. I presume it came naturally to him. If you're having a battle with yourself trying to do something, it can be a battle you might be better not fighting. Similarly, with the likes of Jeremy Clarkson who has written many books. He struck me as being someone who could write a book in a day, he has so many strings to his bow from farming to racing cars to television shows which all comes very natural to him.

Getting things off your chest is always something that all sorts of brain specialists advise to live a stress-free life. For me I took the plunge and I hope people enjoy the read as much as I enjoyed reminiscing on the good things that I enjoyed in life and the not so good things in life that I have forgotten about.

This is one of my columns I did while on a world tour of the west some years ago.

Chapter 23

The Rock 'n' Roll and Gunpowder spirit in Drumshanbo

Last month I went on a world tour of Sligo, south Donegal across the Arigna mountains and ended up in Drumshanbo in Co Leitrim. I booked into the Lough Allen Hotel resort for one night but ended up staying three nights. Drumshanbo has bittersweet memories for me. My father used to go to the fair there to buy cows, I used to go with him. I bought my first calf there when I was 12. I paid £3 for him and six months later sold him for £7, a profit of £4 after EU levies, taxes and other charges that didn't exist at the time. Six years later I went to my first dance in the May-flower Ballroom in Drumshanbo looking for a bit of romance. I met a friendly girl who came from a place called the 'Mountain'. After a few dances and things going well we arranged to meet the following week. It never happened; she didn't appear for our date. I was told by her later that her mother scuttled her plans and mine. The Mayflower Ballroom was a posh place that held over 2,000 patrons. On the night the Clancy Brothers played there in 1961 there were 3,000 there, 2,000 inside and 1,000 outside.

On my three-day tour of Drumshanbo I met up with a lot of positive people who were very proud of their own place and what they had achieved. I met up with Noel McPharland, who along with Seán Nolan, were the men behind the sale and production of Bo Beep jams which was synonymous with Drumshanbo. I first met Noel when he called to Quinnsworth in Stillorgan where I worked many years ago. Despite his low stature he was no push over when it came to selling jam.

In those years Drumshanbo prospered with Lairds Jam factory, Arigna Mines and the ESB Power Station but within a few years all had closed and the Laird factory was empty. They took advantage of their predicament, got up off their bellies and opened up a new mining experience in Arigna that attracts thousands of visitors every week.

The local community under the stewardship of Noel and a good working group got on well and worked as a team. They got a small amount of funding in 1997 to redevelop the jam factory and open a food hub. Today the hub employs nearly 100 people, housing the Drumshanbo Gunpowder Gin Distillery whose sales have tripled in the past four years. There too is McNiffs Boxty which has seen their range of boxty being sold in many supermarkets around Ireland and more staff coming on stream. There also is The Chef in a Box which sells quality, ready-made meals. Noel McPartland Fresh Food Exports still produce Bo Beep jams at the hub. A new state of the art visitor centre is under construction by Pat Rigney of Drumshanbo Gunpowder Gin. Alongside the hub are six other manufacturing units as well as a chef school within the hub. The hub is managed by Fergal McPartland and from my tour they look as if they are running out of space because of the interest of others in becoming part of its success.

When I sat down with Noel McPartland to write this column he started talking and I started listening. After 30 minutes we stopped, and Noel said to me 'Now what questions have you written down there you want to ask me'. I said, 'Noel you have answered most of my questions even though I didn't get a chance to ask you one question'.

I left Noel to do a walkabout in Drumshanbo and my usual surveys of businesses that have closed in rural towns. Out of 59 businesses in Drumshanbo eight are closed, three of them for over 40 years, one bank closed, and one is being renovated. So, effectively there are three closed businesses in Drumshanbo which is only bettered by Adare in Limerick which has no businesses closed out of a total of 62. So, Drumshanbo, after losing its three main employers, didn't throw in the coal shovel or bury their heads in the Arigna coal dust. They took a lead that many rural towns could reignite, the gunpowder spirit approach.

Drumshanbo and the surrounding area has been the stomping ground for many successful business families who made their mark, not just in Leitrim. The legendary JP McManus's Limerickbased successful family came from Drumshanbo and never forgot their roots.

So did the Musgrave brothers who left Drumshanbo in the 1800s and set up various businesses in Cork. Today Musgraves operate the SuperValu/Centra businesses in Ireland, England and Spain. The Musgraves were related through marriage to the Laird family of Bo Beep Jams. About ten miles up the road from Drumshanbo is Cloone which was the birthplace of Pat Quinn who opened the first supermarket in Dublin's first shopping centre in Stillorgan.

In 1959 George Tutthill moved from Mohill to Galway and opened the first self-service supermarket in Shop Street in Galway called GTM. In the same year Cecil Clarke, who came as a shop boy to Mohill, later moved and opened the first self-service supermarket in Navan in 1960. This shows that, regardless of your circumstances, you can succeed with guts and determination and always looking at the barrel being half full, not half empty.

Éamon Daly has been one of the leading lights of Drumshanbo in the world of music and drama. He has played music with Charlie McGettigan. Charlie, who lives and works in Drumshanbo, won the Eurovision in 1994 with Paul Harrington with the Rock 'n' Roll Kids. As a result of their win, the sideshow Riverdance went onto world acclaim as did many other Irish dance troupes. I can only imagine if the Rock 'n' Roll Kids didn't win the Eurovision or weren't well placed we might never have heard of Riverdance or Lord of the Dance. In the world of country music most of you who are my vintage will know of Paschal Mooney, another Drumshanbo man who played all our country favourites on RTÉ 1 for many years.

On my tour of Leitrim, I'm always told good stories. Some of them are unprintable.

One of the better ones was when Noel McPartland went on a trade mission to the Middle East in 1965 selling Bo Peep Jam. He called to a client in Saudi Arabia. For some reason they didn't make jam in Saudi Arabia then. Noel met his Sheik contact to sell his jam. Before he left Drumshanbo he was told by Raymond Laird that there would be a price increase on jam three months down the road which Noel informed the Sheik about. The Sheik told him to just look at the order he was going to give him and then get a price. He then proceeded to order eight, 40 feet containers that comprised of two million pots of jam.

Obviously, Noel had to phone head office the next day to get the best price. He rang Drumshanbo 3 from his hotel room. Operator said, 'No such place'. Eventually, he got through from Saudi to London, to Dublin, to Mullingar, to Carrick-on-Shannon to the exchange in Drumshanbo, where eight hours later Maud Donoghue the telephonist, answered the phone and Noel asked Maud to put him through to Drumshanbo 3 which was Laird's Factory. Maud asked Noel 'Where are you' before she put him through to Laird's. Noel said, 'I'm in Saudi Arabia'. 'You are in your arse' said Maud and banged down the phone. It goes to show the strange things that happen in Leitrim, but they still got the order for two million pots of jam, so a new factory had to be built.

Obviously jams and sugar related products have taken a battering over the years as have many other food products, but it still didn't stop enterprising people from starting things outside the jam pot.

Today Drumshanbo has two swimming pools, one outdoor pool that was built along Acres Lake 60 years ago with top class, well-maintained, outdoor facilities, with the hundred-year-old canal playing host to many cruisers that travel along the Shannon waterways. Across the town is a pool and leisure centre with an outdoor boating, canoeing and fishing marina at Lough Allen Hotel on the shores of the lake. There are four kids' playgrounds which is unusual nowadays with the exorbitant cost of insurance cover for them.

While I was visiting, one of five festivals was in progress. An Toastal, which has been running for years, was the highlight. In the town centre new restaurants have opened as has Jinny's American style diner at Maguires Cottages on the Carrick Road overlooking the lakes and cruisers.

In the town centre a returned 'yank', Joe Gunning, runs Conway's old-style pub and ferries customers home in his taxis and minibuses. An idea I presumed he picked up in his time in New York. Across the street the globetrotting Henry Sorohan, whom I'm told was in more places than Donald Trump, has set up his bar and restaurant. For a town that should have died it refused to do so because the 'Rock 'n' Roll Kids' of Drumshanbo had the guts and determination to get things done and make them happen at all costs, without having to listen to whingers. I admire them for that and give them my award for their inspiration and drive and their desire to look after their great natural resource or everyone.

Chapter 24

Surviving in life and dealing with whingers

Most people have to work to make a living and be happy or miserable. I have known both types of people. People who hated the job they did. It paid good money so there was no way they would leave it. There are others who are mad for money and live a miserable life. Then there are more who are born retired. They never wanted work. They had no interest in work. The job they were lucky to get was that type of job. If you showed any initiative or go in you, you would be told to slow down, you are showing up the rest of us.

I once interviewed a guy for a part time job as a handyman for 15 hours a week sorting bottles, emptying bins and other handy jobs. I asked him if he would be interested in that type of work. 'No way, I cut my finger with a broken bottle once and I wouldn't go next or near bottles since, not even plastic bottles. As for emptying bins, I nearly broke my back lifting a bin once'. 'What about cleaning gutters?' 'Would I have to get up on a ladder'. 'Yes'. 'Jasus, I fell off a ladder once and nearly killed myself'.

'OK, what are you good at?' 'I'm good for nothing'. 'Well why did you apply for the job in the first place'. 'I saw the poster in the window, "handyman wanted", and l live just around the corner.'

There were corner boys around in my youth. People who keep up the building on the street corner. They were part of the 'born retired brigade'. It wasn't my scene. I felt happier working but not stuck up to my arse in a drain where you could see no light or money at the end of it. It didn't last. It couldn't last and I made sure it wouldn't last too long because I hated it.

I promised myself I would never work at a job I didn't like regardless of how good the pay was. I still believed there was no shame in being poor, it was just the inconvenience of it. Having moved on to a job I liked, it became my dream. The money did matter but making a lot of money doing a job you don't like is a waste of time and a waste of a good life. If you like what you do, you will persevere and can do well for yourself. We all have ups and downs, but it is much easier to forget about them and move on if you're busy at what you do.

Working with and associating with positive people gives us all inspiration. Negative people drag you down to their level. Thinking positive and having positive conversations can be difficult in the present times we live in. We went through a lot with wars, threatened recessions, the pandemic and rocketing prices. With all these happenings it can be hard to think straight or think at all.

They say life is for living. We all have our dreams, aspirations and goals in life to work towards, often with stumbling blocks put in our way oftentimes by greedy heartless people. The challenge is to get over or around these and enjoy life as you would like to.

One of my icons whom I have admired for years is Warren Buffet. He is one of the wealthiest people in the world with over $100 billion saved. He is 91 years old. He still lives in the same house he bought over 60 years ago for $37,000; he drives a ten-year-old car. His partner in the business he runs, Berkshire Hathaway, is Charlie Munger, Charlie is 99 years of age. He still has, like Buffet, a razor-sharp brain because he uses it. Their business employs over 500,000 people and is one of the most profitable companies in the world. There is no truth in the rumour that Warren plans to retire before he comes to the age of 95. Nor is there any truth in the rumour that Charlie Munger will replace him as CEO at 100 years of age.

Age doesn't matter much in life provided you're happy. I still couldn't see myself happy at 120 years old though. I'll update you on that at a later date.

During my life I was never led or dictated to by anyone except the people who tell you how you have to do things and the price you pay if you don't do them. I always had enough cop on to understand that. I was always a great believer in listening to people. You learn nothing from talking, you only learn things from listening. My mother's comment to me often was 'You never stop talking'.

Obviously, she was listening to me because she knew what I was saying. I always listened to her and took on board her advice and opinions. She was one of those people who could live on very little even though she was very generous with neighbours, bringing them boxty, brawn and brown bread. She could have just four big potatoes in the house and a few eggs, and she would make eight pans of boxty and eggs and feed all eight of us, including Odie.

Energy costs were nil. Food costs were minimal. Time was of the essence. We cut our own turf, cut our own timber, grew our own potatoes, cabbage, onions, carrots and celery. The wild mushrooms and truffles grew wild in the garden egged on by the horse dung. We got the eggs from our own hens. The caviar we got in the river under the house. Truffles and caviar and now a favourite starter in top class (very top class) restaurants and hotels in the world. The cost of a kilo of truffles now is about €2,000. The cost of a kilo of caviar is about €7,300.

I can't understand how I never went into a business selling truffles stuffed with caviar. Instead, I stuck to the truffle (mushroom) soup and caviar (fish eggs) sambos to help me on my culinary way.

Chapter 25

My life on the road

It's not difficult to remember the ups and downs and the good deals I did, the deals I thought were good deals but turned out the opposite.

I made great friends on the road. People who kept the bread and butter on the table and a few who forgot to pay me. Very few of them I fell out with. I still do business with many of them. Some made it bigger than I did. Some did maybe a bit the same. I still have the greatest respect for all these people and I still keep in touch with many of them and in later years with their children or heirs to their thrones.

Nowadays, the world of business has changed. The days of selling goods out of the back of a Transit van is history. Websites, emails and online ordering now plays a big part in the success or survival of many businesses.

For me I'm still part of the older scene where you do business with people you like, and they like you. I always believe that while the old ways may be sidelined, they will never be fully replaced. My philosophy was always to look after my customers, sell them a good product at a fair price and they will stay with me.

My family runs the business now. They have developed and expanded the business using all the new technology that's available today and gel it with a good, old-fashioned, friendly service. I'm a great believer in moving with the times and I still believe the old phrase, 'Be not the first by whom the new is tried or yet the last to lay the old aside'.

At present many businesses, especially the hospitality trade, have come under serious pressure. It has been building up for years with exorbitant insurance charges mainly caused by fraudulent claims, the smoking ban and drink driving laws. Despite this, we have more alcoholics in the country than ever before because for years you get drunk on €10 a day buying below cost drink in some multinational supermarkets.

For many people in rural Ireland the pub was their local where they met all their friends and neighbours after Mass. A few would meet before Mass. These people might forget to go to Mass but they could tell you what the sermon was about, who said the Mass and who was at the Mass. I'm obviously talking about evening Mass or midnight Mass.

The pub was the only social life for many people of a certain age. You had people who went to the pub every week but never drank alcohol in their life. I didn't start till I was about 19. I hated the taste of the stuff when I first tasted it. After a bit of training and sampling various beers and lagers, I finally found one that suited me and I suited it. That's the way most of us get a taste for anything. Try it first and don't give up.

Obviously, the demise of many rural pubs will have a serious effect on fundraising for the local sports clubs who sold their raffle tickets every week to raise funds for their clubs. Maybe this was on the cards for some time. Maybe we had too many licensed premises in the country for decades. The '70s and '80s were the boom years for the singing pubs. It was a boom year for musicians and showbands in that era.

Dublin pubs were booming for decades. Most of them could charge 20 percent more for drink than their country colleagues. That scene has changed because city pubs are being hit as much as rural pubs.

A friend of mine owned a pub in Dublin for over 30 years. He had a good stand with plenty of money in the area and plenty of noise on the streets around his pub. He once boasted that in the boom times he could buy a house in Dublin from the profit he made in one year. When he sold the pub, he owned ten houses and 200 acres of land all from the profits of selling drink over a 20-foot counter. In fairness he worked seven days a week. He retired because none of his family were interested in taking on his lifestyle. Would you blame them?

The attitude of many young people nowadays is that life is for living and to be happy because money isn't everything. Then again you won't go far without it today and the inconvenience of not having it can cause some hiccups in life.

Throughout Ireland there are hundreds of pubs owned and operated by people in their 70s. Many of them still work six or seven days a week and long hours. None of the young generation want to take over, why would they when they can get a nine to five job that pays better money and much less hassle? There has to be an incentive in every job or business for people to be interested. The days of a publican opening seven days a week and working 80 or 90 hours is on the way out. It was part of life for many in the last generation but the younger generation don't want to know about it.

In future few country pubs will be taken over by a family member unless there is another lucrative sideline with the pub. That sideline could be an undertaking business, a farm, a shop with petrol pumps attached. The days of the country post office being an attraction is gone with the wind. We don't have too many business opportunities to look into to save rural Ireland and we are not working on too many either.

Chapter 26

Travels

We all have to travel and discover new things in life and do new things in life. From an early age I had the travel bug. Myself and Odie were regulars in Mohill. The train used to travel from Dromad to Mohill onto Ballinamore and Ballyconnell. It closed down after I had two or three trips. They closed down many places then. Any places or facilities the British built, we felt we should get shut of them. We dug up railway lines and burned down fine country houses just because it was the Brits who built them. It was a bit stupid. We should have learned from them. We didn't and probably still don't.

I am a great believer in seeing how other people do things well and copy or rob their ideas. The British built the first railroad networks in the world. The Americans and everyone else copied them. They built the finest buildings and canals across the world that are in use to this day.

Some of my travels took me to China, America, Cuba, Australia and South Africa. These are places many people nowadays travel to do business to buy or sell products. It's a small world now and it's getting smaller. Maybe not smaller but easier to get around.

I got a call one day from John Murphy for Castlerea. He asked me if I was doing anything for a couple of weeks. John was planning to go to Cape Town on the Niall Mellon Township Trust building project. I agreed to take the plunge and do something worthwhile for our fellow people, even though I didn't know if I would be given a proper job on the site or a digging job.

I knew the shanty township we were going to wouldn't be flooded. Most of the shanty tents and makeshift tents the people lived in were set up on what was once part of the beach but due to global warming the tide stopped coming in that far at the time. Nelson Mandela was in jail. He got out shortly after and I say it again, there is no truth in the rumour that the first question Mandela asked when he was released after 25 years was, 'Did Mayo win the All-Ireland yet?' You can put that report to bed for now.

The Niall Mellon project got extensive publicity in newspapers and the media everywhere because everyone and anyone wanted to be part of it. In my second year working there I was hobnobbing, eating and drinking with high-flyers from the banking, building, entertainment and media world. Some were hard goers; others should know how to work, and others were so fond of work they would sleep beside it.

I was on the same team as the late Seán Fitzpatrick of Anglo Irish Bank fame. The bank was on a high at the time. They couldn't go wrong. They had big borrowers, big backers and big problems nobody wanted to know about. Seán was a hard goer. I spent a couple of days as his helper on the delivery wagon. We never dropped our guard and we made sure all the trades people had adequate supplies of goods to get the job done. We got helping hands from the locals who were only too eager to help build their community. In two weeks, we built 70 houses that were ready to move into. Not bad for a crew of 400 people, many of whom never lifted a shovel or were ever struck in a drain before.

We did a bit of partying as well as work. We arranged a 70th birthday party for Archbishop Desmond Tutu on the site. A two foot square cake was ordered and we all gave a hand to devour it. I'm not sure if Dessie got a chance to eat even a slice of it. On the job we had an early start. Up at five in the morning to be on the site by 7am. It was the first time I realised there was five o'clock in the morning as well as five in the evening. I had never got up at five in the morning in my life.

In later years I often went to bed at five in the morning.

The early starts did us no harm.

The travel bug had hit me again so I went to Cape Town six times in total. I had met so many people and made so many friends I felt I wouldn't be the first to bailout. We all can spare time in our lives even though we feel we have time to do nothing.

For five years I travelled to South Africa with Niall Melon and various crews to build houses in the shanty towns of Cape Town. In some ways Cape Town is much the same as any major city. It has its share of wealthy people and very wealthy people. They have over six million living in shanty towns which is just one stop up from sleeping in a doorway on the streets of Dublin. Some of the people who live like this want it like this. They don't want to change their lifestyle for many reasons you and I would not agree with.

South Africa has had its share of different governments. From white minority governments to majority black governments. There was never a happy medium so many of these just didn't work. Conflicts ruin any society. It's easy nowadays to create a conflict, especially around religion or colour. For most white people they are happy being white. For most black people they are happy being black. For most coloured people they are happy being coloured. It's the people who cannot decide what colour they want to be – they are the ones who often think there should be racism and conflict.

In our schools' young children seldom think in this way. They are at a stage at five or six they are too young to hate anyone.

Chapter 27

Melbourne and New Zealand

On my first visit to Australia, I settled into a house in Balaclava in Melbourne. It was just a few train stops from the heart of the city with trains every six minutes that cost about 30c return. My plan was to travel around the country.

I started on the Great Ocean Road, on to Castlemaine and up to the Twelve Apostles. I thought the Twelve Apostles was a religious place where the apostles used to go on holidays or on stag parties. It wasn't like that at all. They were 12 standing rocks on the side of the ocean past Apollo Bay. It's Australia's version of the Cliffs of Moher, nothing too exciting about the place, only the fact it's historic and everyone wants to go there.

I didn't get a chance to visit many fancy restaurants because I was travelling by buses and trains. The round trip took me four days and I ended back in Melbourne.

I followed up on some reports I had read about the famous restaurants in Melbourne. One of the top restaurants in Melbourne is owned by Galway native Liam Ganley who, with his wife, owns and runs the popular Fifth Province restaurant and bar, the Angus & Bon and Freddie Wimpoles with local food and foods of Ireland, Australia and worldwide.

Wandering around Melbourne can be a home from home experience. You may not recognise the faces, but you will certainly recognise the Irish accents. I made a habit of visiting the super off-licences around Melbourne. The two biggest are John Murphy's and The Liquor Store who operate off-licences stores that are up to 30,000 square feet with over 100,000 bottles and cans of beer and wines on display. You certainly wouldn't go thirsty on any street corner. Even with the vast number of off-licences, you won't travel too far without stumbling into a pub or out of a pub.

My plan to visit Cairns was scuttled. Over 2,000 miles would mean I would start to suffer from fatigue or jet lag. On my way to Bendigo, I stopped off at Castlemaine. It was a well-known place by many Australians and Irish in Australia. It was made famous by Jack Duggan, the Wild Colonial Boy, who was born in Castlemaine. He became the typical Irish bandit who robbed the rich to help the poor and probably looked after himself as well.

I headed to New Zealand to check out the terrain which I was told was very similar to Ireland. Being a country of similar size and population as Ireland, we have our similarities. Some New Zealanders say the best thing about New Zealand is there are no Australians in it. I don't know for what reason they say that. Maybe like Ireland over the years they wanted their own independence with no interference from anyone just like we believed for generations. It didn't always work like that for us.

Back in Melbourne, I settled down for a few days dining out with my daughter Helen and her husband Hamish from New Zealand. They were well in tune with the hop spots to visit in Melbourne where they served good food.

One of these places, the Le Grande Pizzeria, had won the award for the best pizza in the world. The day after they won the award, they turned out 1,600 pizzas and 600 pastas. It was like a pizza factory cooking world famous pizza which they were churning out of four large, clay domed ovens. The prices were very reasonable for a world famous restaurant, about $16 or €11 for a 12" pizza. To me the pizza was tasty and different, but I don't know why it was the best pizza in the world, just as I find it difficult to understand how awards are dished out in Ireland for world-class food.

That's the secret to success in any business, how to run a successful business where everyone wants to do business with you. In some cases, the patrons may be prepared to pay twice the price for a meal that is cooked or overseen by a catering chef with awards for his or her food. That's the best thing about being famous and good at what you do.

The days of the celebrity fish and chip shops run by Italian families may not have the same appeal even though the fish and chips in these places and others are still top class, just as they have been for generations.

On my second visit to Melbourne, I decided I wanted to see as much of the country and the country way of doing things as I could. I hired a three wheel motorbike with the intention of doing a Billy Connolly style runaround. My intention was to drive to Cairns in the north of Australia. I looked at it like I was going to drive from Castlebar to Belmullet.

I loaded up my goodies, a few bottles of water and the sambo, a map and of course the sat nav and I headed on my way. I was lost after five minutes so I asked Alexa to guide me to Cairns. She was fairly accurate. Take the next turn left and proceed north for 2,500km.

On this journey half of it was outback with no filling stations, no shops, no water to whet my appetite. It was summer and it hadn't rained in some parts for over two years. I had a decision to make. I wondered if I should go or should I stay. Reality prevailed so I kissed my motorbike goodbye and took the Michael Portillo route by train as far as the train went. I then got a plane back to Melbourne dejected and bewildered but ready to start another day's adventure.

At least I did get a chance to see how small farmers with 10,000 acres survived growing vines, while rearing livestock and bees. It looked a much simpler way of doing things than I had to contend with the digging drama in Leitrim trying to get rid of water. They were building drains and dams to hold the water. I could live with that providing I wasn't forced to do it.

Back in the city I was ready to settle down for my few weeks holiday there. The Aussies were more tuned in to the things that Australians did than me. They are one of the heaviest drinkers in the world or so I'm told. They are a brave lot because alcohol is more than twice the price of what you pay in Ireland. They made up for it as petrol and diesel was more than 30 percent less than Ireland. Don't tell them that here or the minister may double the price of drink here just to be in line with the rest of the world. I doubt if they will drop the price of petrol and diesel below €1 a litre but you never know what could happen.

I doubt if they will ever copy the Aussies by deporting people who break the law or steal a neighbour's husband or wife. In these cases, the guilty party may decide to deport themselves for a different reason. Before you contemplate that, just remember Australia is a great country but you can't just pack your bags and decide to live there. There are many varied forms to fill and boxes to tick before you are considered suitable for residence. Many people may not have the stomach for it as it may take up to six years to get all your ducks in order. Telling them you have a criminal record no longer holds any clout in making Australia your permanent home.

On the 23 hour flight to Australia, I swallowed down a couple of sleeping tablets in the hope that I might get a few hours' sleep. It didn't happen. My mind was racing. In the three hours it took us to cross the Sahara Desert I was looking down counting sheep. Three hours of looking at sand dunes. No sheep. Nothing there, only underground oil wells owned by the Arabs.

Talking about the Sahara, I heard about a Mayo man who applied for a job as a lumberjack to cut down trees. At the interview he was asked if he had any real experience of cutting trees. 'I have' he said, 'I spent 20 years working in the Sahara Forest'. 'You mean you spent 20 years working in the Sahara Desert?' the interviewer said. 'Oh,' says your man, 'Is that what they call it now?'

My thoughts were focused on all the Irish who had done this journey by sea. Unfortunate convicts who were transported to Van Diemen's Land for stealing a British landlord's pig or potatoes. I never heard of anyone being deported for stealing a landlord's wife. I'm sure it did happen. Human nature is human.

Australia is a country that runs its own strictly regulated immigration rules. In Melbourne Airport I was pulled aside for questioning. The customs personnel pull in nearly every 50th traveller aside for questioning. They searched my bags a number of times, whisked me down, asked me the same questions a few times. Then they asked me, 'By the way, Mr Kelleher, do you have a criminal record?' Not sure what answer to give, I asked, 'Is that a trick question?' So, my answer was, 'Do you still need a criminal record to get in here?' I was informed that the customs guy's forefathers were part of the convicts who were deported to Australia for sheep stealing.

There were over 80,000 'convicts' transported to Van Diemen's Land (now Tasmania) over two decades to work on the building of ships for the British war machine. The majority of the convicts were from Canada, followed by convicts from Scotland, Wales and Ireland. The minority came from Ireland. Some were elected members of parliament here who were deported for various political offences.

I don't think they do that now. There is no need to as politics is now a clean cut, up front profession where you always have to tell the truth only when you have to. That's life in many ways and it works.

Port Arthur, Hobart in Tasmania is a big tourist attraction particularly for people going to 'tie the knot'. There is a small chapel on the bay in the centre of the compound which is an attraction for newly married couples. There is a flagstone as you enter the 20 seater church with the inscription, 'On this spot James Boden put a hand axe through the head of one of his British minders'. It is on this slab of stone that the happy couples nowadays agree to be loyal and faithful partners till death do us part or until someone with more money or sex appeal comes along.

Tasmania is now a more civilised country mostly inhabited by Tasmanians and Chinese. It became an infamous place for us Irish because we learn all about the bad things that happened there.

Despite that, it was the birthplace of our world famous actor Errol Flynn. Errol's grandfather worked in my own parish as a blacksmith in Lough Rynn. He was sent voluntarily to Tasmania to train blacksmiths to make gates, fencing and shoes for horses. There were over 2,000 blacksmiths at the time. It was an easy trade to pick up at the time as many of the convict's forefathers perfected the trade. Errol Flynn's father John became a professor in the university in Tasmania while he went on to be one of the most famous acts in Hollywood. To this day he is remembered by many old and young in Tasmania, New Zealand, Australia and many parts of the world as well as in my home parish of Gortletteragh.

Chapter 28

Being a celebrity in Melbourne didn't suit me

Before I left for my tour of Australia a friend of mine gave me a contact name who was President of the Australian Football Association in Melbourne. I contacted him when I arrived there. He was a true blue Australian who was very involved in Australian football and on the committee along with another 20 people. I was invited to an after-match function as a guest. I certainly wasn't prepared for the celebrity status they were going to afford me. I was told to come to the event dressed respectably with a suit, shirt and tie.

I am a bit like Elon Musk. I usually wear an open neck shirt because, over the years, self-indulgence in fine foods and wines, means most of the shirts I now own don't button on the collar. I bought a tie on the way to the function. I slapped on the tie and headed to the door of the reception at the MCG Stadium executive suite, togged out in my suit, collar and tie. As the top button would not close on my shirt, I was forced to keep the pressure on my tie, so it stayed in place. As I shook hands with the 20 or more celebrities who came to greet the celebrity from Ireland, I was forced to drop my guard and let go of my tie to shake hands with all the people who bowed to me. I was told before I moved to tighten up my tie and button my shirt. I couldn't do it without choking myself.

I moved on to the next area, and I was still holding my tie against my chin to comply with their strict dress code which I thought I had mastered. The next staff member to approach me had a different request. When I thought I had ticked all the boxes, I got a tap on the shoulder and a whisper in my ear, 'Would you mind buttoning up your fly?' Embarrassed and in shock, I was forced to turn my back and make amends for my absent-minded behaviour. It wouldn't happen in Ireland simply because I was never classed as a celebrity that needed to conform to rules. It was a great learning process I will remember for a long time for all the wrong reasons. I'll know better the next time.

Melbourne's MCG Stadium has over 40 bars and restaurants within the stadium. People arrive long before matches start with all the family and settle down to a day of eating, drinking and enjoying themselves. I stumbled out of the place after six hours of burning the candle at both ends and, in the middle, as well. I think I was more able to manoeuvre the steps and turnstiles than most. The Australians have a great ability to consume quantities of drink and hold it without losing the run of themselves and running riot.

The next day I was travelling by train to Apollo Bay. There was no available seat on the train, so a young lady got up and gave me her seat. I suggested I was okay, and I would be happy standing up for the short journey. She explained to me why she gave me her seat. If a young person does not offer their seat to an auld buck like me, they can get a $100 fine. Amazingly this lady gave me her seat which I accepted. To me this system is not what one would expect but it made me aware about what respect and consideration for older people is about because young people in Australia do it because it comes naturally to them. This would work anywhere and be appreciated by all.

Chapter 29

Strikes and shortages

Going back to the late '70s and '80s there was a serious shortage of some essential products, mainly caused by industrial disputes and strikes.

One year there was a strike in Dublin bakeries. Bread was being smuggled across the border to the supermarkets in Dublin. There was no shortage of flour, buttermilk, salt, bread soda or any of the ingredients needed to bake a good home baked cake. The supermarket shelves were full of the stuff but very few wanted it. They would prefer to go hungry than start baking over a hot stove. They got accustomed to buying their favourite slice pan or batch loaf so they would queue for two hours just to get a rationed loaf.

Soon after that there was a shortage of gas and diesel. I'm not sure if it was another strike or the Arabs holding back supplies until the prices went up. I used to cross the border into Fermanagh and fill my tank with petrol. On the way home, I would buy a few boxes of butter. It was half the price in the North at the time so I could make a few pounds on the smuggled butter. That became a bit of a disastrous business for me.

During one summer I packed six boxes into the boot of the car. I spent the following two days doing my rounds, calling to my customers in the pubs. It was mid-July and very hot weather. I forgot about the butter. When I went on my rounds in Leitrim selling the butter to my friends and neighbours all the butter had melted in the summer sun over two days. That put an end to my butter smuggling forever. It just wasn't for me, and the profit was very small.

Petrol shortages lasted for weeks, even worse than nowadays. You had no mobile devices, apps or modern technology on the art of survival with no petrol.

I was stranded in Mountbellew at the end of November. No petrol to get back home. I booked into a B&B for the night. To amuse myself and drown my sorrows I went to the pub. There was a card game on which I put my name in to play in. There were three turkeys as prizes on the night. Being a lucky guy, I won one of the turkeys. Little did I know the turkey was alive when I went out the back to collect my prize turkey. I was in the manure business again. No petrol to bring me home and a 23 pound turkey for company on my rounds till I made it home. It wasn't a great experience or a pleasant smell in the car either. Regularly I had to bring the turkey for a walk through fields to keep her active and fed.

Four days later I got home. Turkey in tow. She was as delighted as I was to make it back to a place where one could have peace of mind. Sadly, my prize turkey had issues. She wasn't used to a confined space like a car and obviously wasn't happy even though she had her two or three meals a day. It didn't work out well for my Christmas dinner either. The stuffing was the only stuff we could eat. Unfortunately, her legs were black and blue like she was in the ring with Mike Tyson from rolling around the car without a seatbelt on her. We had to resort to a rasher and a boiled egg for the Christmas dinner so a non-merry Christmas was had by all.

Chapter 30

Growing up

Life was great in the '50s. You knew all your neighbours. They all spoke to you on the road, and they came around to the house whether invited or uninvited. You didn't have to get an invitation to anything except a wedding. You just turned up with one arm as long as the other. There was always something in the house to feed them. My mother was a dab hand at cooking. She could muster up a meal for all of us with four potatoes and four eggs. This could feed the nine of us, including Odie.

She boiled four big potatoes, mashed them, added some milk, onion and the four eggs. She then baked it on the fire. It was my favourite any day. We never went hungry. My father used to kill pigs for the neighbours. No money exchanged hands. He got the giblets, the liver and the heart. He got the pigs head complete with ears and eyes. My mother made home cooked 'brawn'. It was a treat to eat and to give it to our neighbours.

Sometimes my father would get the legs and tail as well. There wasn't much meat on it, but it was tasty in a homemade caviar sauce with truffles. The truffle grew in the garden egged on by a supply of horse dung. The caviar (fish eggs) we collected in the river below the lane. The fact that the pig's tail had so little meat meant my mother used to advise my father by saying, 'The next pig you kill for someone, will you cut the tail nearer to his feicin' head and cut the head closer to the tail'. It seldom worked because my father usually got a few shots of whiskey as well which more than compensated for the work that was involved.

All of my friends at school were sons or daughters of famers except for a few. There was a doctor from Africa living in Mohill and one of his family came to our school. At that time racism wasn't invented. As far as I was concerned there are only two races and colours of people in the world. Black and white. I later found out there are black, white, coloured, Indians and Hispanic and they all look different.

There was a family of 'tinkers' camped at the sandy banks over the road from us. Myself and Johnny were good school buddies. On my way back from Sorohan's shop I would stop at the canvas tent they lived in on the side of the road. The father would be making metal pongers (mugs). They always had a roaster of a fire down that could be seen for a mile across the fields. They weren't into climate change then. There was no need to be because we were all told to look after the things God gave us.

Johnny Stokes was in my class. We walked the roads or fields back from school. He always referred to himself and his family as being 'tinkers'. Dare you call him a 'traveller' or 'itinerant' or a 'gypsy' or any of those fancy names the do-gooders of the world like to change every decade for some unknown reason, even to the ordinary tinker.

Having a black child sitting beside you didn't get tongues wagging. Rafa's father was from Africa. He was black. I was from Leitrim and white. So what? All that changed when do-gooders came on board to put a spanner in the works for all of us and the world as well.

Nelson Mandela summed it up well when he said, 'I don't care whether my cat is black or white provided she catches mice'. That's my view and I think everyone should take the same approach except the animal lovers who feel we shouldn't kill mice but it's okay to kill a rat. Strange world, strange times, strange people.

Chapter 31

Lord Leitrim and Frank Cunningham

Lough Rynn Castle and Estate, the house of Lord Leitrim, is now a high class, popular hotel. A great range of trees from around the world still adorn the surrounding walled gardens that roll down to the lake which is now home to many water sports. Most of the lakes and rivers around there were once hubs of lake and river fishing. In Lord Leitrim's time you were not allowed to fish the rivers without getting permission. Today we are back in the same situation where you are not allowed to fish many of our salmon waterways. So much for the words of the song, 'Only our rivers run free'.

At one stage Lough Rynn estate had over 100 people working there, mainly made up of blacksmiths and stone masons. At that time every building and wall was built to last. Even the cattle sheds and outhouses were built to last. Today all of the schools, churches, houses and the castle built there over 100 years ago are still standing after many years of neglect.

The British perfected many of the great things we still have in life. They built the railways, canals, imposing castles and bridges and we in our wisdom decided over the years to burn them down, close them down, dig up the railway tracks and abandon the canals that many European countries developed further to attract people to the waters to partake in water sports and what is regarded as the biggest sport in the world, fishing. Sadly, many people in authority often replicate the things others get arseways and fail to look at how well people do things.

Colonel Gadhafi, when he took power in Libya from a corrupt government, revolutionised Libya, a country made up mainly of deserts with no water. Within a few years he brought water to every household by digging a canal to bring water from the ocean through the country. Similarly, he developed their oil reserves and with the revenue from the oil the country became self-sufficient. The world didn't like his ways of doing things. Europe, in particular, was not too happy either. They wanted rid of him. France with the backing of the coup with NATO initiated his downfall. Gadhafi was in the process of getting many of the nations around him in the Middle East to form an alliance to get its own currency. This if it happened would do untold damage to the French Franc at the time as the Franc was the main currency in these countries.

As it turned out the French Franc disappeared when they joined the EU and as they say, the rest is history. We are now back in a world where we are trying to cope with similar bigger issues with Russia and China than we had with Cuba or Libya.

A couple of miles over the road from us lived Frank Cunningham. He was a sort of a corner boy who hung around the streets of Longford and Mohill. He was a hardy buck.

He left for England when he was in his 20s. After a couple of years, he was called up to join the British forces in the war. He refused to go so he was arrested and forced to go to an army training camp. It was a tough place. During the winter they were forced into the exercise yard to train in the snow with no clothes on them. At night they were forced to live and sleep in cells with rats running around. This was total hard labour which he found hard to cope with. Rather than be left there indefinitely, he joined up.

He joined up against his will. Six months after joining, he got a relative of his in Ireland to write to him and say a close relative had died in Ireland and he should come home. He was allowed compassionate leave for two weeks. They gave him two new suits, two pairs of socks and two pairs of underpants and he headed for the boat at Holyhead. It was all a set up, so he never went back. He hung around home for a good few years.

I used to meet Frank on the road to the pub. He was a mind of information. He never married but he used to have more women than Henry VIII had. That was his claim to fame. In Sorohan's pub he would meet up with some of his mates who had spent time in America.

One neighbour, Pete Joe Wall, used to drive a fancy car. He found it hard to know the difference between first gear and reverse. He would either hit the railings at the pub or shoot across the road and mount the ditch. The two front wheels would be up on the ditch or in a drain spinning.

The boys would go out to try and move the car off the ditch onto the road, again under protest from Pete. He would give them instructions to leave him alone, telling them, 'For Jasus sake guys, I drove a snow plough in New York for 28 years'. It was a different job, shifting snow off a driveway and shifting his car from the top of the ditch. Things normally worked out well and they all got home safe. By the time the car got lifted back onto the road, there were another four or five piled into the car for the lift home.

Frank and Pete, the two returned emigrants, lived out their bachelor lives back in the neighbourhood they left 50 years before. At least they had some place to come back to instead of maybe ending up homeless on the streets of London or the streets of New York. They were the real characters who never lost their accents or the love of their own place. Pete got a bit of a pension from his years in America. Frank got no pension. If he hadn't deserted the army, he would be entitled to one. If he went back to collect even his belongings he would have ended up in prison. Luck was on his side because he had something to come back to.

Chapter 32

Paddy the postman

Paddy Kelly had less than half an acre of garden around the house. Locals used to 'wind' Paddy up on his rounds delivering the post. A neighbour told him that a lot of people were getting agricultural grants for keeping cattle, horses, ponies and fowl. Paddy contacted our local TD at the time to make an application for the grant, saying he was keeping livestock on his lands. When the inspector arrived to check his holding and his stock, Paddy had four ducks in the back yard and a pony that strayed in from our land. He didn't get the grant, but he nearly did because he was a staunch Fianna Fáil man who put up posters and roared his head off after masses at election. He was well into Fianna Fáil.

He knew all the politicians in the area – good ones and useless ones. Paddy, being our postman, was 'a man of letters'. I once suggested to him that he should write a book on Fianna Fail because he was so well in, or so he thought. His answer to my suggestion was, 'I have a pair of kneecaps and I want to keep them' and he had enough money in life with a good pensionable job as a postman. He didn't want to put his life in danger by telling tales from school that shouldn't be told in public. Things have changed since then with Twitter, Facebook and social or anti-social media.

Paddy was never married. His only cost was to feed the four birds in the garden. The pony was sent packing the day after the inspector called.

Paddy's left hand was a bit deformed. He had a hole in it from being shot in the war. He had a job to do every night or early in the morning. He used to clean the wool or cotton from the sheets and blankets that often drifted into the hole. He used to use a knitting needle to do that job. It never seemed to bother him. It used to bother me looking at him doing it.

They used to say that Paddy shot himself in the hand so he would be discharged from the army. I think that could have been true because he had the casing of the bullet that shot him. The only way he could have had that was if he disarmed his attacker. Anyway, he lived with the hole, and it didn't bother him.

Paddy wasn't a great cook. He could just about boil an egg and burn a rasher. I once asked him, 'Why did you never get married?', his response was 'Why would I get married?' 'Well,' I said, 'Wouldn't she cook a bit for you?' 'She would,' he said, 'And she would ate half of it'. Enough said.

He used to wear the medals that he got during the war or ones he picked up at car boot fairs. He had them sewn into his pockets or they were hanging off himself. His pockets were filled with junk and application forms he got from the department for grants he applied for. Once he had a bad tumble off his bike. The doctor said at the time he would have had much worse injuries only for the fact he had so many medals wrapped around himself along with the old army uniform.

Most of the time when he got into bother it was on his way home from the pub with half the letters from the previous day still not delivered. Every letter he delivered to us, he could tell us who sent it. He knew and remembered the writing and he knew the stamp on the official letter from the guards requesting you renew your dog or gun licence.

For some he was the only contact with the outside world for a week or two depending on how close you were to your neighbour or how long the lane you lived in was. One neighbour lived across the fields from us but by road it was six miles and then they had to travel in a mile long lane with potholes and blackthorn bushes that would take the head off you or take the eye out of your head. Everyone who visited them went by travelling through the fields and bog with a flash lamp so as to avoid bog holes and drains. You followed the light in the distance. It was your only guide.

Chapter 33

The 40 shades of grey

I was always obsessed with certain colours. I think most people are. They either like or hate a certain colour. The forty shades of magnolia or white I was never fond of. My favourites were the old colours we used to see in old country cottages and pubs years ago. They had a mix of red, burgundy or black mixed with white on the walls. The old red window cottage with white walls always stood out. People would often paint the door and walls on the barn the same colours because they had it left over in the tin.

Today, the variety of colours for cars are endless. Some years ago, I bought a new car. The colour was a new colour for cars, it was a cross between chocolate red, brown and burgundy. Nobody knew what colour it really was or cared. I couldn't really explain what the real colour was. On the brochure it was colour code MS66531H. That's an easy enough colour to remember and understand.

At the time a friend of mine told a friend of his, 'Kelleher got a new car'. The friend asked him what colour it was. He said it's a wine colour. 'Very good,' said your man. 'Is it red or white'. It was neither. It was brown.

Today's world of colour, colour schemes, kitchens, bathrooms, bedrooms have taken on a whole new lease of colours. Gone are the magnolias and whites. They are being replaced by 40 or more shades of grey, from dark grey to nearly white green. Is this a ploy to get us to buy more gadgets for our home or is it just the way we are? Let's hope they don't decide to change traffic lights to grey, blue or wine colour. I'm confused enough so I would prefer if we just stuck to the few colours we always had. Then again Johnny Cash was the first to write and sing about the Forty Shades of Green, which we can now add to the forty shades of grey, white, red, blue, lavender and lemon. Once you are not colour blind, it's easy to recognise every one of them even if you don't really know the flavours or colours of them. My next car will probably be 40 shades of green or yellow.

Chapter 34

Pubs in rural Ireland

In every shopping mall, shopping centre and town centre, while the authorities were trying to curtail drinking, there was more alcohol being consumed. The supermarkets started price wars with drink – beers, lagers, wines and spirits. They sold them as 'loss leaders' (below cost price) to attract customers.

Alcohol became the biggest turnover of money for many supermarkets. The government kind of lost out as they were taking in less taxes on off-licence drink than drink sold in the trade in bars, lounges, hotels and restaurants. The government obviously saw the opportunity to make big money by allowing multinational stores to sell drink at below cost.

They changed their tune somewhat because of the problems cheap, uncontrolled drinking was causing in society and because of an outcry from many people. It didn't work because some retailers can find ways around selling drink at below cost even though it's banned.

Today the hospitality business, not just pubs, is fighting for survival, trying to cope with energy costs and the many other hidden costs associated with running a successful business. Then there's insurance costs and fraudulent claims that insurance companies don't always contest. They may just pay out and the business is told the outcome a few weeks later or when they go to renew their insurance. The government is 'looking into' this for over a decade now with no real action. Crazy stuff.

Maybe over the years we had too many pubs for the amount of people who live and work in the country. There are still a lot of bars/restaurants who are still doing good business because they moved with the times or things didn't depend on bank loans to keep the business going.

Businesses everywhere, except the illegal businesses, are under serious pressure in town centres and rural areas. A survey done nearly 20 years ago showed Ireland had roughly the same population as Manchester. Despite that Manchester had 65 percent fewer shopping outlets than Ireland. So, judging by that we should have a population of 17 million to justify all the retail units we have. That could happen within the next few years if present events continue. That's for another day and a job for fellas with more letters after their names than me.

Chapter 35

Thrill-seeker

Growing up I probably wasn't much different to many other kids in rural Ireland or kids in towns and cities. We all got up to our own devilment. I was a bit of a thrill seeker. I always went for challenging stuff. I was often told I should have been a stunt driver. I took gambles climbing and swinging out of trees. I fell out of one once and broke an arm. I didn't learn a lesson because I later fell off a building and broke a leg. Another time I was downed off a ladder and broke most of my ribs. To me they were challenges I didn't plan. Most normal people don't go out to do these things.

Living and growing up on a farm will have its ups and downs. It's a place where you are not afforded the hygienic systems you have in a town or city home. There were sheep, cattle and fowl always around you. They weren't too concerned where the toilet and washroom facilities were located. If you left the front door open the hens or ducks would make the kitchen their spot to sit around. Obviously, cows, sheep or horses would not be as cheeky. In many homes in these early years young pigs, after they were born, would be placed in a basket beside the fire to get them started off in life so they would live a healthy life when they returned to their mother in the pigsty. Amazingly pigs are animals that are easy to train, even to potty train.

On a visit to Hong Kong, I was intrigued by the pets that people walked around with on a lead. I noticed what I thought were black and white dogs on leads in the city. On further investigation I found out they were pet pigs. These pigs are popular in many parts of Asia and China. They live with their owners in a 40 story block of flats. The only way I was sure if these pets were dogs or pigs was their behaviour. Pet pigs or any pig will find his or her way around by hitting their nose off the ground while the dogs will find their way around, like the rest of us, with the head up in the air looking around.

There are many types of attractions in the country and on a country farm that can occupy an active mind for hours. I was obsessed with water, lakes and rivers. I should have formed the Green Party. There was so much happening in our lakes and rivers. At that time, they were full of fish, frogs, swans, otters and many other watery creatures who travel the earth unnoticed. We had salmon, trout, eels, pike in the 360 lakes that are scattered around Leitrim. Like many of our people who emigrated, the salmon went back to America and Alaska. Modern fishing methods and quotas don't allow them past Newfoundland or Rockall anymore. They seldom come back here to get asylum even in a place they were born in.

Drains, rivers and lakes are places that grow a lot of weeds and other vegetation that birds and fish live off. In modern Ireland it has been used for the last 100 years as an excuse not to clean our lakes and rivers. This gives rise to lakes and rivers 'rising' and flooding half of the west of Ireland. This is put down to climate change. A good answer but it's not the right answer because farmers and anyone who got planning permission to build a house on a water plain or in a swamp will not be too enamoured with that situation. We were lucky – our house was built on top of a hill. The Shannon would need to rise by over 1,000 feet before we had any fear of flooding. The only thing we owned was the land at the bottom of the hill and that's where our trouble started or ended up.

To me it was a great challenge ploughing through flooded fields with the green grass visible under my toes. The swans had the same thoughts as I had. Over 100 of them would arrive to feed. Once the flood arrived, the snails and any other earthworms would crawl out of the ground for air or so as not to get drowned. The swans were there when they surfaced out of the ground into the water. To the swans and seagulls, that was their caviar sandwich meal.

The thrill I got ploughing through the fields of water with my friends didn't go down too well at home – a bigger fire had to be put down to dry all the wet clothes. The story didn't end there. When the floods left, I was left at a loose end. No more thrill-seeking activities around. I had to create my own. I headed for the drains and shores that were all around. The ducks had found them long before me. They had them well irrigated before I got there.

They would be out ploughing through them early in the morning foraging for earthworms and any other delicacy that may have wandered into them. When they took off, I took over complete with my bucket, shovel and small homemade wheelbarrow. That was my workplace for two or three hours covered in muck, doing a job that went nowhere. To me it was the greatest excitement in my life. It was the freedom and excitement of not being told what to do. Nobody could see me because all the drains were at the backs of sheds or trees.

People haven't changed much since. I have grandsons who have copied my wayward way of getting enjoyment out of life, doing simple things in life ploughing through muck and dirt and the more muck they have on themselves, the more exciting it gets. Amazingly my granddaughters don't go down the same mucky route. Maybe again if my parents bought me computers, laptops and mobile phones then I would have a different outlook on what enjoyment was all about. Then again if we all had those opportunities, then we would all have ended up as scientists travelling to the moon to sort out the drains and dust that's up there.

It was never my dream to be in a job like that where 90 percent of the time you were talking about things that happened in the world a million years ago or what will happen in the world a million years from now. I don't want to know as I guess I won't be around.

Maybe I will. I could be reincarnated back into this world as a cat or a pet pig in Hong Kong. If that happens, I won't be too interested in science or science fiction. I'll probably still want to do the things I did when I was here – cleaning drains, sitting in flooded fields or rubbing muck on my torso just as pigs and other wild animals like to do. Please God I won't be reincarnated as a crocodile. I might not have a choice.

Chapter 36

The good, the bad and the hungry

There were times in the flat in Dublin when money was scarce on Thursday, two of us might have to eat the one egg. This taught me how to survive in a crisis. At one stage in my life my mother would be in the same scenario where she had to make ends meet. She would boil an ox tongue slowly for about four hours and then slice it. My father wouldn't be impressed with ox tongue. He would ask my mother, 'What's for dinner today'? 'Ox tongue' she would say. 'Jasus,' says he, 'You don't expect me to eat something that came out of a cow's mouth?' 'Okay,' she said, 'I'll give you a boiled egg so.' Enough said.

Down through the years I always had a great interest in cooking. So much so that I might sit up half the night watching people from China, Korea, Taiwan or Hong Kong produce the finest street food in the world. They have perfected the art of cooking classic dishes with eggs, cheeses, vegetables, noodles and herbs. Today the Chinese eat on average one billion eggs a day. Ox tongue isn't one of their gourmet foods. Healthy eating is all about home grown, healthy foods. That's their philosophy and it works. You seldom meet a 20 stone Chinese man or woman so they must be doing a lot of things right.

In Ireland we never got the inclination to start up too many street food stalls. Maybe it's the weather, maybe it's the EU regulations that most countries in the EU ignore and do their own thing. We in Ireland are not bold boys and girls. We stuck by the EU rules when it suits and that's most of the time. Maybe we have gone a bit over the top on many things while ignoring things that have a much more serious impact on us and our economy. I'm afraid I'm not going to change the rules.

We are now in the middle of a recession or there could be a worse one on the way. Prices are rocketing so we will all need more in our pockets or we need to spend less to make it go around. We are told there is nothing that can be done about inflation. The only way to counteract it is to spend less. You can't do that. We all have to eat. One person I knew had his own plan in place when petrol went up in price. He decided to do as he always did. He put €20 of petrol in the car every Friday. Regardless of how much petrol went up, he was putting no more into it. So, his approach was, 'When it's gone, it's gone'. It might be the approach that most people who came from the same Ulster county take but it doesn't always work like that. Sitting in your car on a border road with an empty tank may not be a pleasant experience.

Tightening your belt is one thing but discarding your trousers is another. You have to eat, drink and drive to work to make a living. Running down a country road to catch a bus to bring you to work and bring you home is literally a non-runner. We are not at that advanced stage in Ireland just yet. Recessions come and go. Prices go up and never come down. Politicians will promise you the sun, moon and stars but you will have to go and collect them yourself. Despite all these advantages and disadvantages, we won't stop whinging. Why should we? What would we have to talk about if we did. The weather, the war and when will Mayo win the All-Ireland. These are the questions that are hard to get answers to simply because we live in a world of uncertainty that we probably never want to get out of. If and when we do, all our dreams will come true. The waiting will be over and unlike Cavan people who still reminisce about the great Cavan teams that won the All-Ireland in the '40s and '50s as they look towards New York and wonder if it will ever happen again.

Chapter 37

The local well

At school I had a reasonably happy time. The teachers didn't give me too much hassle or me to them. The fact that they knew that I got up most mornings early to milk three cows before I headed off to serve Mass was a plus. If they didn't know this, I let them know. Before I headed off to school, my mother would give me a bucket to collect a gallon of spring water from Michael McKeon's spring well which was on the way from school. Michael McKeon was a returned yank who built his galvanised home in the middle of a field with no road or driveway to it, just a path through the field to the front door. Our well used to run dry in the summer but McKeon's well flowed from the hill through the rock before it reached the bottom of the lane and into the well. It's still there and many of the locals still come there to fill milk cans or five litre bottles with the water. On the way from school, I filled my bucket which had a lid on it.

Before I filled the bucket I usually lay down on my belly and sucked the water out of the well. It would have been a bit awkward trying to drink water out of a galvanised bucket by holding the handle. Regularly Tommy Joe Duignan's horse would drink from the overflow drain from the well. They say the best creature to judge the quality of water is a horse. They won't drink stale or stagnant water or they won't drink tap water. They only drink fresh water that came from a spring in the ground. Obviously, they are better at preserving the planet and the healthy options than many human experts are.

Even on the warmest day of summer, the water was cold in the well. I still go back to fill up my plastic container. To me it was our only source of fresh water before we got tap water in the house. It left a lasting memory on me for a long time and inspired me later to write a simple poem about the simple things in life.

McKeon's spring well

I sucked the water from Mc Keon's spring well
While spiders rushed to the sides like hell
No HSE scares or water bugs, they weren't even dirty words.
Throughout our young lives we drank the best
It was nature's way of doing the tests

It supplied the townlands all around
It was the greatest treat to cool you down
With a steady flow from the hills above
It just wasn't a place that you hung around

For through the fields we were forced to go
Through long wet grass and sometimes snow
We were always blessed with an abundant supply
That never seemed to ever run dry

In summer times the moss grew around
While the grass sprung up along the sides
More spiders and frogs lived around the place
They always seemed to stare you in the face

Those days are gone forever more
Contamination and slurry has played its role
It was part of the simple life we lived
With nourishment flowing from Mc Keon's top hills

– Oliver Kelleher (2009)

Chapter 38

The downside of modern technology

Everybody in life is out to better themselves. Nowadays we all want to live in a good house with all the mod cons. From satellite TV, smartphones, new apps and technology that will do everything for us, well nearly everything. Starting in the '90s the biggest luxury many people wanted after they built a house was a new set of electronic gates. They became the 'in thing' to stop cattle that broke out on the road from ploughing through your new manicured garden. They stopped any unwanted visitors to your home.

Sometimes they were a nuisance, sometimes they were an asset when they worked, and you had the code to open them. In some cases, it puts friends off coming to visit you. Then again there was no reason for them to call as they could easily communicate with you by smartphone, text or any of the new social media gadgets that now take up many people's lives, many of which I haven't got around to testing out. I think I am allergic to them because every time I try them, they seem to be allergic to me and they fight back as if I was an alien trying to destroy them.

My first disastrous encounter with modern technology was a few years ago. A friend of mine built a new home. I was invited a number of times to visit for coffee. I took the plunge one day and headed out the country to visit my friend. It was my first visit. I arrived at the driveway. It was a long driveway, and you couldn't see the house from the road. The house and garden were guarded by electronic gates. I didn't have the code, so I phoned my friend to let me in. Problem was he couldn't find the app to press the button to let me in. The gates were seven feet high. Instead, I started to climb over the four foot metal spiked railings around the gates. Disaster struck. I got impaled on one of the spikes with one leg inside the wall and the other outside. I couldn't move backwards or forward. The only option I had was to make a dive for it. In doing so I fell in on the grass but not until I ripped the trousers off myself because that's where the spike got stuck. I then walked up to the gates, and they opened for me. Unfortunately, I was not in a visible or fit state to sit down and have coffee in anyone's house with both legs of my trousers ripped off. My only option was to get back in the car and head for home. One hundred yards down the road I pulled in, composed myself and decided to write a poem on my escapades and how new modern technology can muck up our lives.

Electronic country living

Over the wall you try to get in
To say hello, to your next of kin
The cameras shine on your face below
You curse and swear with a few loud roars.

Keeping up with the Jones's is a different thing
When you lock out your neighbour behind the screen
You may feel posh, and you may look cool
To a friendly neighbour or a child going to school.

The money was there, it was part of the scene
That locked your friends from your private dreams
When the batteries run out and you're on your own
You're feicin' neighbours, they're not at home

It was you who planned your way of life
For privacy, swimming pools, you can blame the wife
They were there to monuments of better times
When banks were loaded, till the well ran dry.

The cows stroll in from the farm next door
They dig up the garden of grass and stone
All me flower beds are looking crap
For me electronic gates, they have failed to work.

– *Oliver Kelleher* (2009)

Chapter 39

Writing and free speech

For over five years I wrote an opinion column, firstly with *The Connaught Telegraph* and later with the *Western People*. My writing approach was always to be fair in the comments I wrote. I never criticised the people who operate many systems that can go pear shaped because of political interference. They are the issues I felt I needed to be highlighted. Now and again, I would be approached by people who had issues with what I said. I had people approach me to tell me the things that I should have printed. I was often classed as controversial for whatever reasons most couldn't tell me.

Regularly I was approached by people who had a great story, many of which were unprintable. The most exciting stories I got were usually in the pub with drink involved. We can all be experts on many things with drink in us. For years the printed press was the only way many people in rural Ireland had to stay in touch with the outdoor world – who died in the area, who was up in the court for everything and anything illegal or a row with a neighbour. Today, the world of communication has been taken over by social media and apps. Some of the new technology has created a lot of problems for society because regulators turn a blind eye to the whole idea of free speech which the print media cannot print.

We now live in a world where we all feel we should be entitled to free speech. Often when you print what may be fact, you can be sued. This only applies to certain sections of the media. Similarly, with derogatory words like the F word. You are not allowed to print it in a family newspaper, but you are not banned from using it on a family TV show. Depending how famous a celebrity you are depends on the number of times you can use these derogatory words on TV and radio. Many people often asked me where I got the inspiration to write a column every week. It was a bit like asking me how I got the inspiration to talk as much as I did every day. Nobody ever asks a politician how he or she got the inspiration or the memory to talk about so many things, especially the things we all want to hear.

Oftentimes I would wake up at four in the morning because something was taking over my mind and I couldn't sleep. Once I jumped out of the bed and put pen to paper. I would have 1,800 words written within the hour. Once I got back to bed, I was out for the count in a minute. The next day at 12 o'clock I would try to read what I had written eight hours earlier. The biggest problem I had was I couldn't read my own handwriting in the column I had penned simply because I had written it so fast and left out the odd word or spelt the words incorrectly or half wrote the word. It was my way of getting things I felt strongly about, felt sad about or felt happy about that gave me the inspiration to tell the world what I wanted them to know and appreciate.

Nowadays every celebrity feels they have to write a book or two. From Jeremy Clarkson to Charlie McGettigan to Bono everybody likes to tell their story. It's a great way to know and understand you. My favourite read for many years was Con Houlihan who wrote a great column in the Evening Press. I have always avoided criticism or controversy in life, business and writing. It was never my way of life and I never had any intention of upsetting anyone.

Now and again, I met people who made comments to me about something I wrote where they had interpreted it in the way they wanted to interpret it which wasn't the way I had written it. Up until a couple of years ago, I never read a book. I never had the patience to get stuck in. In the past two years that has changed after starting and finishing a couple of interesting books that I think may have been written especially for me to read.

Maybe when you enter the golden years, you feel you may need to catch up on things you never tried before. I get a lot of inspiration from two of my icons, Warren Buffett, now 92 and his partner in business, Charlie Munger, 99, who are still at the coalface and work every day overseeing their $300 billion empire. There is no real need to have to stay working till now as they are valued at nearly $200 billion between the two of them. Amazingly nobody ever asks them when they plan to retire. I think Buffett said recently that he planned to write another book. If that does happen it might put the pressure on Charlie to write his memoirs too.

Chapter 40

Religion and growing up

Fr Peter Murtagh was our parish priest for about six years when I was growing up in Leitrim. I used to serve Mass for him, fodder the cattle he reared on the land around the church and the school. In the summer I would wheel the turf for him. He was a slave driver on the bog, but he paid me for every day's work I did. His sermons at Mass would frighten the shite out of all the auld ones who weren't too sure where they would go after they left this life. His sermons were fire and brimstone jobs. What you can do and what you shouldn't do and what you cannot do. For most of them in the church it went in one ear and out the other. I took it all in with a grain of salt. After four years of serving Mass I could nearly recite the Bible off by heart. I heard so much from kneeling on the Italian marble kneeler in front of the altar that was later to give me pains.

Tommy Warde, my neighbour, never missed Mass. I don't know why he bothered his arse going because he would give me lessons on religion on the way home on Sunday. He would say to me, 'Hi young Kelleher, do you believe that our Lord was able to walk on water when he met up with his friends, all of them fishermen on the lake in Galilee, do you think he could turn water into wine? He would be a big hit with the publicans if he were around in these tough times and the bit about him rising from the dead'.

Warde was a bit skeptical of all this, but he had to be a believer like every other race and creed in the world who believe in some sort of God whether he be black, white, coloured or Indian, male or female. I'm sure the people in Africa didn't believe in a white God just as we didn't believe in a black God. Scientists haven't established if Jesus was ever really born to the Blessed Virgin Mary.

In the past we were lucky we weren't crucified if we even opened our traps. There are many stories that are told about religion and religious beliefs. I heard a few years ago about a lady who was married to a 'bit of a waster'. She tried her best to change him but with little luck. She went to counsellors, head experts and do-gooders who advised her to bring him to somewhere religious where he might see the light. First, she brought him to Lourdes. He never stopped nagging all the way there and back and worse he got when he got home. Then she brought him to Fatima hoping he would see the light. Nothing good came out of it. Then she took him up and down Croagh Patrick thinking she would wear him out or wear him down. It didn't work.

As a last resort the head shrinker suggested she bring him to the Holy Land. Flight booked, a few pounds each way on Ryanair. He never stopped complaining on the flight. Arriving in the Holy Land, tragedy strikes. They disembarked at the airport in Jerusalem, and he cocked the toes and died. Panic set in. She was all alone in a foreign land with no friends. She contacted the local undertaker who arrived quickly. He gave her the options to sort out the situation.

Option one was to bury her nagging husband in the Holy Land where he would be buried in very sacred ground where many saints and scholars were buried before. The price was €3,000. She nearly collapsed at the price and asked for the breakdown. One thousand for the coffin, one thousand for the grave and one thousand for me, he said.

Option number two was to ship her husband back to Ireland. The cost was €9,000. In shock still, she asked for the breakdown.

'Three thousand for the coffin, three thousand for shipping the remains back to Ireland and three thousand for me.'

'What do you think?' asked the undertaker. Without hesitation she said, 'Ship him back'.

'But why do you make a silly decision like that which will cost you six thousand less to bury him in the Holy Land in a sacred grave where all the holy spirits have been around for centuries, why are you so stupid tell me?' he asks.

She composed herself, looked the undertaker in the eyes and had her say. After years of heartache and pain she had enough and proceeded to tell her story to the undertaker. 'You know sir, a long, long time ago ye buried a fella here and in three days he rose from the dead and I'm taking no chances. Ship him back to Ireland.'

These are some of the things that can happen in love and war.

Chapter 41

The flu that changed the world

At the end of 2019, the world was getting a bit iffy. I was touring Australia and New Zealand when it broke that a new flu type symptom was taking hold in some parts of the world. It didn't cause too much concern until early 2020 when it started to spread.

With the world now more up to speed on what's happening and what's not happening via social media, Facebook, Twitter and all the other apps and methods of spreading news fast, we were all made aware of what had hit the world.

Donald Trump put the blame on the Chinese. As far as he was concerned that's where the virus started. Obviously, it had to start somewhere. Pinpointing exactly how it started became an impossibility for scientists, politicians and people in charge of world health.

It was the greatest upset to my cosy, little life and many other people's lives that had ever happened before. The cause of the panic, the pandemic, caused lockdowns and the shutdown of business. Everyone now became experts in the field of medicine, pandemics and the main causes. We had to believe scientists and politicians. Obviously, you have to because they are the people who run the world. For two years we were living in the land of wonder and wonderland. In a world where it wasn't safe to be alive. Don't put your snout outside the door or you're a goner.

I was out and about delivering sanitiser and other hygiene products which were in high demand during the pandemic. The roads were deserted and businesses closed up in lockdown. Only essential services operating like off-licences, supermarkets and others. Every pub in Ireland was closed. As a trial they allowed certain pubs that served food to open provided they sold food. The experts believed if you sold a burger and chips in a pub for €8.50 you would be unlikely to pick up the virus. It was a novel idea never tried or tested anywhere in the world before. We are not sure if it worked as the scientists and experts in the field haven't given us an update yet.

At least one thing they did establish was that the main place you could pick up the virus was in the pub guzzling pints at the bar, hugging and kissing your friends you were drinking with the night before. I wasn't into that auld hugging and kissing hence I didn't get the virus. I could have got it in the off-licence, but I didn't because I'm not a man to visit these places too often as I seldom drink at home, only tea, coffee, milk and water.

For over two years the cursed virus took over our lives with legs added on. There were amazing stories, some sad ones told about the virus. One person told me he had the virus for over 20 years. The symptoms were pains in the back of his legs which he had for 20 years. This was one of the symptoms of the virus. His long suffering wife told me she had the virus for over 30 years. The symptoms she had was a 'pain in the arse' from listening to her husband complaining about something every day for the 30 years they were married. A pain in the arse I believe was one of the symptoms of the virus.

For the two years, I spent some of the time looking out the window, going for walks with the imaginary dog I don't have or lying out in the sun on some tropical island drinking bottles of champagne so the alcohol would kill all the bad things that had built up in my system. I didn't do any of these because my mind was racing, my head reeling and my stomach growling. I settled down to writing poetry and staying in contact with people. That's the way William Butler Yeats used to do it, lock himself in a room, look out the window at the world and get his inspiration. For more inspiration he went on tour around Sligo and up to Dublin to visit and stay with friends and stay for extended periods. I didn't do that because nobody wanted me near their house, let alone staying with them for a prolonged period.

I got my own inspiration from YouTube. I'm not on Twitter, Facebook or any of those fancy gadgets that will tell you everything about the world and what's happening in the world.

With a bit more time on my hands, I started reading books. I bought several books and got several books as presents over the years. I started most of them, read the first 20 pages then skipped the next 260 pages and went to the last twenty pages just to get the punch line. I just didn't have the patience over the years to sit down and read a book. The problem I had then was I was a slow reader and a fast writer. I probably wrote this book by freehand in less time than it would take to read it. The only reason I read these books was because I went out and bought them myself. As a rule, if I get a book for free I don't usually have much interest in it. So, the two books I did buy myself I did read because the contents were of interest to me.

I got the writing bug a few years ago just to get things off my chest and when I felt some things had to be highlighted. I didn't change the world even though a lot of people who read my columns in the *Western People* and *The Connaught Telegraph* did agree with where I was coming from and what I was saying. Not everyone agreed which was understandable because everyone has their own views on things, including me. Whether you're right or wrong is immaterial, provided you don't upset people by telling mistruths about them which I made sure to always avoid.

During the lockdowns I took to a bit of comedy writing, quotations that are relevant and catch phrases and stuff that may make people think about, laugh about or cry about. I had planned to write 200 of these and put them into a book. The problem was after I had completed the 200, I couldn't stop and as and from this moment I have 4,000 of them. They started off as one line, then two lines and then up to six lines and still no book completed. Maybe that could be my next project.

Most of us are now back to normal living. The pubs are open again and the ones that survived the lockdown are still in business. Others didn't open because of the hassle involved in the jump start. Anyway, the off-licences are booming so the people of the world won't die of thirst in the foreseeable future.

The shutdown

Two years ago, the music died
The pubs and businesses shut their doors
The off-licence opened to better times
For take outs

Despite the fact many places were closed
From lockdown, panic, pandemics and more
The old got shaken, the young didn't care
If pubs or businesses never opened again

Stories took legs across the land
Of people dying in the crazy lockdown
We lost sight of the sick around
Because we couldn't care for them
Only in corridors or on hospital grounds

Our vital services ground to a halt
No bed in a hospital was your lot
How dare you complain or raise your voice
We have other more important jobs on hand to fight
People died in corridors or at home
No point in complaining if there's no bed available

Today our minds have all forgotten
What's still a problem across the world
The panic ends as life goes on
As life has to function in every type of world.

– *Oliver Kelleher* (2022)

Chapter 42

Cops and robbers

I got to know one of these people briefly in Dublin. He was a born liar and robber all his life. He was a career criminal who did several stints in jail over 50 years and broke out of jail as many times. He specialised in smash and grab raids on jeweller shops in Dublin in the '40s, '50s and '60s.

He ended up as Ireland's most wanted man in 1948 after a raid on a premises where a sergeant got shot dead. He was classed as a kleptomaniac, which is a serial robber. It's a disease that there is no cure for. Ireland is still full of these people but in today's world they are known as shoplifters which sounds more to the point. If you tell a judge in court, you are a kleptomaniac he/she will take a different view than if you said you were an ordinary decent criminal who was stealing a few groceries to feed the children.

Shoplifting has become a more serious, well-planned trade compared to the smash and grab era. Most jewellers' windows don't have easy access because most have toughened glass and steel window grills and alarms. The days of robbing an engagement ring to start the process of marriage has changed. You may need to put a bit more up front to woo a lover for life or even for a couple of years until the stars go out of the eyes and the divorce papers arrive.

It's now common practice in many parts to change the partner a couple of times in your life. Americans are specialists at that, for many reasons. The days of throwing back the €300 ring are gone. They say that marriage is grand, but divorce can be 500 grand. Then again, I always believe money was meant to go around, not to be hoarded or wasted. Wasting or losing money can have many long term effects and implications. Losing it is much worse than wasting it.

One night in a pub a guy comes in and walks up to the bar and calls the barman aside. He asked him a question. He said, 'I was drinking here for a couple of hours last night, do you have any idea how much money I drank?' Apparently when he got home, he realised he could have mislaid some of his money. The barman responded, 'You drank well over €100'. 'Jasus,' says your man, 'that's great, do you know I thought I lost it'. At least it made his day as he had drunk the money and he didn't lose it as he thought. You always have to keep your eye on the ball and your eye on your money because the world is full of thieves, robbers and people around who may even steal your pints when you're not looking straight or talking sensibly.

Chapter 43

When inflation deflates you

Inflation is probably now the dirtiest word in the English language and it's the most confusing word in the English language depending on who is discussing it and how they discuss it. We hear all the glamorous comments like 'we have inflation under control' and the following day all the toll roads of Ireland increase their prices by 15 percent.

With things like this happening, everything that has to travel by road from anywhere in the world to Ireland and around Ireland will automatically go up in price because of the decision of one or two individual companies to increase their prices because of inflation. What can we do about it? Very little except stop travelling on toll roads and take to the side roads. That won't happen because time is important when trucks or vans are delivering goods around the country.

It's easy to get confused over these figures. Earlier this year we read reports that the eurozone inflation rate fell for the first time in 17 months. When you read the article that's not what it says. It says that the annual rate of inflation across the entire eurozone area 'eased' back to 10 percent in November 2022. This was the annual inflation 'easing' over 17 months, not the annual which is 12 months. This was classed as a 'flash' estimate from the EU's statistical agency Eurostat, which could also be classed as creative accounting.

The figure compares to the annual rate of 10.6 percent recorded in October 2022 and it's the first fall in the rate of inflation in 17 consecutive months. The report and the accuracy of it is a lot like the weather forecast, which can be confusing – hit or miss or miss and hit. That's the way we live our lives in Ireland right now. Is it a similar scenario in other countries? Or are we just another crowd of whingers who are worse or better than the rest of the world?

Maybe we are a race of people who like to offset everything we read or hear to make things more confusing? Many reports in Ireland hinge around politics. If a politician says something it is often interpreted as gospel truth and we don't question it. We take it as the truth and at face value until you hear the real story. If you ever hear the real story you may have, by then, forgotten what the first story was and therefore the real story may be of little interest.

I never got too involved in any political party. I had my own things to deal with in life and business and politics could make or break you. You're often better to paddle your own canoe. One has only to look at Sam Bankman-Fried from FTX Crypto Currency exchange. He pumped millions of dollars of donations into the American Democratic Party. It didn't work or he didn't get enough time for it to work. The $32 billion company was gone wallop before the Democrats had changed the donation cheques. There is nothing worse in business than getting a dud cheque.

I remember shortly after I started in business, I got a cheque returned from the bank with the words 'Refer to Drawer'. Being a bit naïve, I asked a friend of mine in business what these words meant. He explained it in simple terms. Fold it up, put it in a brown envelope and put it in a drawer in the house safely. It's still in the 'drawer' after 35 years or more along with 20 or 30 more.

That's all about taking gambles with people you trust and don't trust. We are all told you shouldn't take gambles in life. That sounds great, but if you don't take gambles, you won't succeed. Taking a gamble with someone you don't trust can be a big gamble and I would be inclined to steer clear of these types of people if you can.

Honesty, dishonesty and liars come in different forms. You can meet a lot of them. Many dishonest people may change with the wind. Honest people usually stay the same. Then you have the people who tell a tall story that sounds good but in fact is a pack of lies. That's why an exciting lie is better than a boring truth.

Nobody likes to be called a liar. Usually, these types of people get an array of more colourful names that often don't offend them. Dishonesty is a different ball game. You can usually spot a liar fairly fast. A dishonest person can get you on their side with soft talk and promises. When you fall for it, you may be much more out of pocket than listening to a liar. We all know that what causes many people to be in these categories is money and greed. For some it works out well because they have perfected the art over many years.

Chapter 44

Life's ups and downs

I was never one to worry too much about myself. I was always more concerned for other people's welfare than I was about my own. Any upsets I had in life I moved on or tried to move on to better times and think about all the positive things that were happening around me. We all have upsets in life such as when a family member is sick or a loved one passes away.

My wife Mary passed away long before her time. After Mary passed on, I met up with Lillian McNicholas. Lillian ran the Beverly Hills bridal shops in Castlebar and Galway. We were very good friends and partners for a number of years before she passed away before her time too.

The reality is these things happen to everyone. For some people their crosses can be much worse than others. For some life can be so cruel. This can be caused by things you have no control on. It can be caused by yourself and the lifestyle you had that you may be unable to change or handle. Digging oneself out of a rut can be a battle at times. I have great admiration for someone who can do that and start again.

Money can play a part in luck, especially if you're starting a business, buying a house or rearing a family. You cannot survive without money even though it is often classed as the 'root of all evil'. Too much money as a rule is not a good thing unless you know how to handle it and how to distribute it. It can cause serious upsets and disputes in families for decades. We have all witnessed the disputes in families over land and property, over who didn't get what. There was never any dispute in my family that I knew of. My father passed away in the '60s so my mother automatically inherited the farm. When she passed away in the '90s she had a will left in a stocking. What all six of us got was in six brown envelopes. My brother Aiden got the land because he was already farming it. She divided her fortune out evenly between the rest of us.

She left £1,200 to bury her. She left the balance she had saved, about £1,900, between the rest of us, about £380 each. That was her life savings. She was happy having just that because she could live her life happily without much money. You didn't need a lot of money in those days if you grew your own potatoes and veg, reared your own hens and ducks and killed your own pigs.

In the bottom of the stocking, I found another brown envelope with my name on it. I opened it and found a few crumpled up pieces of paper. One was a reference that the parish priest gave me when I left school. The other was my Leaving Cert results.

This was my first time studying them or even reading the results. I studied the results more than I studied for the papers. I wondered back, what if I had stayed in the drain as my father had told me? Would I have dug a hole down to Australia? Would I have ended up in the tunnels in England or would I have become an oil well tycoon out in Texas or Russia?

No one knows. Not even me. There are opportunities around every corner. We all have to look around these corners and choose to take up a job that you will enjoy. If you enjoy it, you will probably be good at it provided you stick at it and get the lucky breaks.

Often people would tell me I was lucky in business. My response was always the same, 'the harder I worked, the luckier I got'. Then again, I knew people who were never too fond of work and still did well for themselves because someone else who worked for them created the wealth. No successful business can stay successful without good loyal customers and dedicated staff who are interested and happy at what they are doing and I was always lucky to have these people around me.

Over the years we all have ups and downs, misses and near misses. I was no different to most. Maybe a bit worse than some. In my young years I crashed the odd car where I overshot the runway because I wasn't concentrating on where I was going. It's one of these phases in life most youngsters go through. I had to cope with a few mishaps and health scares. None of them bothered me too much. I looked at spending a spell in hospital as a learning process and as a time to chill out, reshape my mind and come up with new ideas for my business. These events never worried me too much and today I have put all this negative stuff to the back of my mind. I can't ever remember what year I was laid up or how long I spent in hospital. My approach was if you worry you die and if you don't worry you die, so why worry?

Regularly I meet people who tell me of the times I was out of commission because of some upset or another. Some people remind me of these events so they get a chance to tell me their sad story. Once I met one of these people. I asked him, 'how are you doing?'

His reply was, 'I'm lucky to be alive, I got a suspected heart attack?'

I asked, 'What's a suspected heart attack like?'

'By Jasus if you got one, you would know what it was like.' He clicked his index finger and his thumb and said, 'You could be gone like that.'

I still didn't know or understand what a suspected heart attack was. He either got a heart attack or he didn't get a heart attack. I didn't probe for any further gruesome information in case I got too much I couldn't handle.

I often think and act as if I'm going to live forever. My aunt Bridget lived to 100. She had a great life, always in good humour with a great hearty laugh. She was often asked if she had any regrets in life. She said she had one regret and that was if she knew she was going to live to 100, she would have 'looked after myself better'. My mother had the same attitude. She never feared aging simply because she had done all the things in life she wanted to do and achieved all the things she wanted to achieve. It's a good approach in any walk of life. She always believed there would be no trailer behind the hearse.

Regardless of how famous you are in life or what you have achieved, once it gives you the buzz to do that is what matters most. The financial reward is immaterial. The only comments you hear about people when they pass on is what they achieved and did for mankind, not the money they left to mankind to squander.

Chapter 45

What's cooking?

When I first thought about writing a book, I wasn't too sure what to write about and what people would be interested in reading. I had my favourite memories that I wanted to write about, like cooking, the stock market, making a small fortune buying and selling shares and losing a small fortune. Writing about my travels always appealed to me. The adventure side of it, the trills and the near misses I had in various places.

For most of my life I loved cooking and trying out various foods in different formats. Today I still get stuck in sometimes against the wishes of my family members who may get sick of me trying to do 'my' recipes. My boxty recipe on the RTÉ Heat programme was, I think, the first time boxty and black pudding was served with apple sauce and a side salad. It's available in many places today and boxty has become somewhat a celebrity dish even though most people who order it don't know what they are eating, except the people of Leitrim who were reared on it. Amazingly, dishes like this and many other simple dishes with two or three ingredients are often the best sellers.

On YouTube the meals that often get the most hits are dishes cooked with the humble egg. Dishes like French toast, various types of omelettes or simple scrambled egg recipes. To me, these I would class as idiot proof cooking because you can cook up many of these in less than ten minutes and it can be hard to make a 'balls' of it unless you take your eye off the ball or off the pan. Nothing worse than an overcooked omelette or a hard boiled roasted egg that the water has boiled out of. I did it a few times in flats in Dublin and elsewhere. It's not a great thing to put on your experience reference if you are applying for any job that you need to be tuned into.

Today we have a greater variety of foods than we ever had. We can cook up the finest healthy food at home or in the thousands of restaurants across Ireland. We are up there with the best in the world. Twenty or 30 years ago the main topic was often about junk food. Today there is more junk stuff in the world than ever. We still have junk food which we don't talk about too much. Nowadays, we have more obese people in the world now than ever before. Obesity is now a symbol of who you are. You can no longer tell someone they are overweight, not even your dietitian can tell you it would be no harm if you lost a few pounds.

Junk has taken on a whole new meaning, not just about junk food. I often hear people referring to someone's house 'being full of junk'. These are places where people hoard rubbish that they think will be valuable. In later years we hear of junk mail, junk bonds and the junkets that operate all over the world. This whole lingo would mither you, leaving you unable to put any perspective on life, living, obesity and weight. That's some of the trials and tribulations of living in a world where our eyes and egos are bigger than our mouths and stomachs when it comes to eating or work-outs.

Chapter 46

Fidel Castro's Cuba

Cuba always intrigued me. It always had a bit of an Irish connection because of Fidel Castro's connections with Che Guevara whose ancestors came from Galway. Fidel Castro's Cuba was similar to Ukraine of today.

The Americans put all sorts of sanctions on Cuba because of Castro's close ties with Russia and other communist states which led to the Bay of Pigs landing of American troops in the harbour with the intention of scuttling Castro. It was a disaster for them, and they were forced to retreat after Russia said they would send fighter planes to support Castro. From then on Castro did his own thing and ran his country as a sort of a communist state with a bit of freedom to do most things except visit America. America, in response, banned flights to Cuba.

I went there in the '90s with the intention of meeting up with Fidel. It didn't happen. I was told he was in hospital at the time. In his youth he was an icon among his own people, a bit like Volodymyr Zelenskyy is in the Ukraine today. On my arrival in Havana, I was greeted by not too many dignitaries even though a man whose ancestors were born down the road from me was a regular visitor to Cuba in the early days to support Castro and his regime. Errol Flynn was a regular caller who stayed with Castro and tried to convince the Americans to be good boys and play fair with their near neighbours, which can be a hard thing to do at any time, even to this day. When we look at Putin's attacks on the Ukraine and China's manoeuvres around Taiwan, we all see what can happen or could happen. We are now back to that era where everyone is afraid to intervene because the world is full of nuclear weapons that could wipe us all out with the touch of a button.

Cuba is not a place where you will experience all the fancy shops, restaurants and pubs we have in Ireland. It still is, or was then, living in the '50s. I stayed in a hotel in Havana. It was an iconic place. Al Capone stayed in it in the '20s. I was told Marilyn Monroe slept in the bed beside me. Not really. I was in room 236 and it read on the wall of the next room 237 that Marilyn Monroe slept there one night. I didn't meet Marilyn either. All the celebrities were long gone.

On my second week there, there was a red alert warning that a hurricane was on the way and there would be a curfew for three or four days where you weren't allowed to put your snout outside the door, let alone go out. It was my first experience of a lockdown. It was good training for what was to happen to all of us when the pandemic and lockdowns hit us in 2020. I spent three days in lockdown in Havana eating bananas and nuts. I couldn't stay in hibernation.

When the worst of the high winds and rain subsided, I headed to the promenade. It was deserted. Still high winds and 20ft waves crashed into the promenade wall across a six lane motorway. I was forced to take refuge in a 20 foot container that was bolted down on the street. The two workers who operated out of it couldn't budge. We were rescued by the police and taken home to isolation. When the hurricane which they named Ike at the time passed, the world opened up again, the sun shone again. Restaurants and bars opened and the 1930s gambling jazz music erupted in hotel lobbies, lounges and dining rooms.

I had planned to move out across the island to see how ordinary peasants, who were boycotted by America for half a century, survived. They survived like we did 60 and 70 years ago in the country with ten sheep, eight hens, a cock and a few cattle where we were nearly self-sufficient eating boiled eggs, boiled bacon, roast chicken, pan fried boxty and boiled boxty.

Today Cuba has sort of faded from the limelight with the passing of Castro. It's no longer a place where the Americans flee or care about even though you can now get flights from America to Cuba. It's no longer classed as a serious ally of Russia. They have moved on to build their own economy by staying friends with people who matter.

The day my Leaving Cert results arrived

Posing in my ballroom days

The original Ballroom of Romance in Glenfarne, County Leitrim

Left:
My first reference, from our parish priest, Fr Peter Murtagh in 1960. It says, "I have much pleasure in stating that Oliver Kelleher is a u. good boy, the son of a u. decent small farmer with a big family."

Myself and Mary's wedding day. From left: My brother Mel, my mother Annie, myself and Mary, my sisters Bridie and Rose and my brother Aiden. Front, from left: my nephew Tommy, niece Jackie and nephew John.

On their double wedding day on 1 June 1942, from left to right: Pat Flynn, Annie Flynn (née Kelleher), Paddy Kelleher and Annie Kelleher (née Reilly). The wedding reception took place at the Kelleher Estate, Drumgrania, Mohill, County Leitrim. The honeymoon was spent in Dublin. They stayed in the North Strand Hotel and North Strand was bombed that night by the Brits. Was there a matrimonial lesson there?

The first Leitrim Association in Mayo dinner dance. *Pic: Karl Keaney*

Myself and my flatmate John Reynolds in Dublin in the 1970s

My father and mother with my sister Bridie and brother Mel. I am in the middle looking after them.

Right: Sister Cecilia presenting a cup to the Leitrim Association in Mayo. The Ballinamore GAA club was named after her father, Seán O'Heslin.

The trail-blazers: Gortletteragh – Leitrim Senior Champions 1970.
The 1970 Leitrim Senior Championship-winning team, with
trainer Hubert Reynolds, which paved the way for the future
progress and success of the Gortletteragh club. Had the club
not won in 1970, one wonders what future there might have
been. The team set a very high standard to follow. Back row,
from left: Mel Sorohan, Charlie Shanley, JJ McGarry, Joe
Sorohan, Mick McKenna, Paddy Kennedy, Seamus Colreavy,
Oliver Kelleher, Tony Collreavy and Benny Kilkenny. Front row,
from left: Michael McGarry, Paddy Reynolds, John McKenna,
Jack Colreavy, Mick Keane (captain), Mickey Dorrigan, Gerry
Moore, Joe Canning and Brendan Muldowney. Inset: Hubert
Reynolds (trainer).

The first meeting of the Leitrim Association in Mayo. Back row,
from left: Jim McGarry, Oliver Kelleher, George O'Toole, Martin
Moran, Mick Devaney. Front row, from left: Ben Wrynne, Mary
Kinelley, May Moran and Jim Short

Making a presentation in 1986 to Mick Devaney, a fellow Leitrim man exiled in Castlebar

Meeting Seán Quinn at his book signing in Mulveys in Carrick-on-Shannon

Myself and Mary with our four children, Helen, Sharon, Sinéad and Ronan

Left:
On tour at Powerscourt waterfall in the 1970s. Mary and myself at the front with our friends, Joe and Rose Canning

Right:
My wife Mary with Billy McLoughlin in 1976. Ivor Hamrock is in the background.

Left:
My wife Mary making a presentation on behalf of the staff to Maurice Flynn, Mayo county librarian, on his move to Limerick

Right:
My daughter Sinéad with her husband Ger and their children, Maia, Anna and Ben

My daughter Sharon and her husband Brendan with their boys Ollie and Luke and girls Kelly and Leah

My daughter Helen with her husband Hamish and their children
Isabelle and Lewis. They live in Melbourne, Australia

Right:
My son Ronan and
his partner Carmen

Below:
My son Ronan and
myself

Cooking boxty at Castlebar Heritage Day in the 1980s with Tom Dempsey - he provided the sausages

The pony that couldn't stay at home

Left:
Gifts Supreme on Linenhall Street in Castlebar

Right:
At the official opening of our Gifts Supreme on Linenhall Street, Castlebar in 1989 are, from left: Pádraig Flynn, the then Minister for Environment; my mother, Annie Kelleher; my wife Mary and myself

Left:
Don't I look stylish?

Our showrooms at Moneen, Castlebar

With my patented Insignia glass, which was a very successful product for my business

I'm pictured here with Mick Morgan, who was the face of the Insignia glass campaign

I made a presentation in July 2007 to former Polish President Lech Walesa during his visit to Mayo. Mr Walesa, as head of the Solidarity Union in Poland, was centrally responsible for the collapse of the Iron Curtain and the Soviet Union. From left: Lillian McNicholas, myself, Michael Horgan, director, Rehab Group, Lech Walesa and Joe Kennedy, chairman, Ireland West Airport, Knock.

Relaxing in Venice in 1970

Right:
Myself
and
Declan
Murphy
in South
Africa
with our
two
minders

Left:
The local
tavern we
frequented
in the
shanty
town in
South
Africa

Building houses in a South African shanty town with the Niall Mellon Township Trust

Right:
Children at the Niall Mellon building site in South Africa

Left:
A children's crèche in Cape Town

Myself and Keith Duffy of Boyzone in South Africa

Left:
A board meeting in Cape Town

On the ground in South Africa

Sketching an artist in Cuba!

Right:
Myself, Willie Scott, Patsy Fadden and Paddy Burke

I was forced into action in the 1990s when I had to take charge
of operations on the frontline at the Warsaw War Museum

My return visit to Woodstock with Gusty Murray and a friend

Chapter 47

Burning the candle at both ends and, in the middle, as well

Starting a business, you know nothing about how big a big gamble it is regardless of how big the bank that is backing you is. You may be one of the lucky ones if you can employ good people who know the trade and knows the market well. Down the years I have seen this happening many times where businesses that had great potential floundered. In some cases, the bank that gave them the money collapsed as well. The latest collapse in cryptocurrency and crypto trading has been a typical example where these businesses are dropping like dominos because the experts who started them and developed them didn't know what they were doing. They made a lot of good decisions but they made more big mistakes that brought their house of cards crashing down on them with billions in losses for hedge fund investors and bankers. It may be an expensive learning process when you are not prepared for it. The fall from grace can affect one person more than others depending on how long you were running the business. They say, 'you should always stay a decent person regardless of how successful you are because you may meet the people you met on the way up when you are on the way down'. That's when you know who your friends are.

It's a thin line between making a success in a business and a failure. It's not something you want to think about when you start a business or in running a business. It could wreck your head. You could spend your life wondering why you were such an idiot for ever starting. It's not a great approach to take to anything. Obviously, you want to like what you are doing to succeed, you need good, loyal staff, and you need good, loyal customers. I have to say I always had those.

Over the past two decades in Ireland, we saw some of the power names in business and banking collapse. Strangely most of the people blamed everyone except themselves. That's a trait many people who feel they can do nothing wrong usually resort to. They say, 'if you think you know everything, you have a lot to learn'. We all have a lot to learn all the time. That's why I believe you learn a lot more from listening than you do from talking.

I learned a lot over the years from listening and I lost a lot because I was listening to the wrong type of talkers who had only one agenda on their mind. Their own. That's often what makes businesses exciting and costly. I don't have an issue with the mistakes I make myself, but I do have issues with people who forced bad advice on me that cost me money. In one case a stockbroker advised me not to invest money in a stock against my own gut instinct. The same issue I had with the same broker six months before where I asked them to 'go ahead' and buy the shares, even though they had thought they had convinced me not to buy. So, I lost out because the shares went up and they hadn't acted on my instructions. Second time around when it happened, I had lost out on a five figure sum. They denied that I had ever booked to buy the shares. After a number of efforts being made by me to get proof against one of the big boys, I finally got a copy of our recorded message which clearly stated my position and they were forced to pay me the money.

If I had made the same cock up and denied it, I think the treatment I would get from the law would be somewhat more active. That's why you can often have a battle on your hands even when you're right. Over the following ten years things got better in some ways and worse in others. There was no point in living in the past because there is no future in the past. Like everything in life, some days are diamonds, some days are stone.

There are times when you can talk your way into trouble. A friend of mine some years ago did that literally. He tried to settle a row outside the Cloudland Ballroom in Rooskey. He ended up with a black eye and a swollen lip. When I asked him later what happened he told me he was talking when he should have been listening. Fair comment. I think he got the message in the wrong way. That's when you know who your friends are. Some will have sympathy for you. Others will say, 'weren't you a right bollox to get in-volved?' We all learn things when it is too late. In some cases, we can go back and make the same mistakes all over again.

In business it's impossible not to make mistakes. The important thing is you don't make them too often. Now and again, I made what I thought was a mistake and it later turned out to be the best mistake in my life. Over the years some of the best deals I did, I was told at the time I was stupid. Normally if you go with the flow and follow what every other 'expert' in town did, you couldn't go wrong. If you did your own thing and used your own gut instinct another set of 'experts' tell you that you are mad simply because no one else would do that. Some years ago, I did a deal for a prop-erty investment that I was told at the time was an unbelievable deal until I started to dig deeper into it. It seemed an unbelievable deal until I started asking personal questions about it. I said to my ad-viser that it looked too good to be true.

Normally if a story is too good to be true it usually is and as it turned out it was too good to be true even though it was backed by the government and a developer who went guarantor for €100 million. It was an era in Ireland when everyone spoke in millions. If you didn't have millions the banks would give it to you. As things turned out the guarantor for our €100 million went wallop owing €600 million. I lost the property even though I paid in full for it with interest and service charges, management fees and govern-ment levies. That's when the people who told me at the time about the cute hoor I was changed their tune and comments to, 'weren't you the right bollox?' I was a bollox. If I had walked the other way I wouldn't have got caught by the soft talker and soft money the developers got from a few gullible gobshites. I have no regrets though. Nobody died.

If I got all the promises again, I might make the same mistake. Some people class that as 'greed'. Maybe it is. Then again if you never take a gamble in life, you may achieve little. Even not taking a gamble doesn't mean you are not greedy. I know some very wealthy people who never took too many gambles. They became wealthy in other ways or by letting other people take the gamble for them. There is no excitement doing that, but you can accumu-late a lot of money that you don't know how to spend. The bottom line is that someone, someday will get their hands on it and they will get as much or more pleasure spending it as the greedy miser spent saving it. That's why you're better off to be born lucky than rich. If you're rich everyone is after your money, and you're only remembered for being famous. Famously wealthy. When you die, they often want to know where all your money went.

If you're born lucky you get a different breed of people surrounding you at race meetings, at football matches, in the pub or anywhere your luck can run out. If you stay happy and healthy it doesn't matter too much. If you're struck down with an illness where you cannot work, your whole world of luck and money changes. Oftentimes no amount of money can change things for the better. At times like that money becomes the least of our worries and luck becomes our main concern to get well and survive. I've seen it all happen around me and I still believe if I had my life to live all over again, I would live it all over again, but I would make a few changes, not too many.

Chapter 48

Time to take stock

When you have time on your hands and time to think you can learn a lot of things provided you can remember that a lot of the stuff that goes through our minds are probably stupid things we don't want to remember. I usually glance through these things fast and move onto things that are of interest to me.

The two things I read up on and study most are about cooking and the stock market. I have a repertoire of menus for dishes from Hong Kong to China to Taiwan. Most of them, probably 500 of them, I would never get around to cooking, let alone eating them. Like things that interest you, it's good to know about them and know you can cook them anytime you please. It's not something you have to spend too much money doing unless you burn the arse out of a saucepan or the coating off a good pan.

Dealing in stocks and shares can be trial and error. Often more error than trial. To me it's like dealing in farming stock, like cows and calves. It can be very difficult to know when you're up, down or out because markets change so fast. It's a gamble, just like anything in life. A couple of years ago I watched a programme on RTÉ about Seán Quinn, who was Ireland's biggest employer, running a highly successful company.

Seán always had the real Irish entrepreneurial touch about him. For some strange reason Irish politicians don't often like these types of people. They often prefer to try to put them down. They seldom work with them to make Ireland a greater place to work and start a business. They take the same approach to Michael O'Leary and Ryanair. I often think they would prefer it if it weren't one of our own who started up and ran these businesses. They don't feel it is good practice to talk to these types of people for advice on how to bring more business to Ireland and match the skills and get up and go of these people who had a lot to offer. These people, like many, are gamblers because you don't know from day one if you're going to make it in business. That's the gamble.

Seán Quinn spoke about gambles he took and he said he was just as keen to win his game of 25 with his 50c a head to play as he was about his big deals. Amazingly, most of those involved in the media spoke about what he did wrong and how it would have panned out if he had done things differently. Would he have saved his empire? Did the media care if his empire thrived or collapsed? Would the same people or the politicians care about the demise of Ryanair?

Hindsight is a great learner. We can and should all learn from it. Sometimes we don't. If we did fail and decided never to go back into business again because we made a lot of mistakes and maybe two or three small ones, we would have no gamblers in the world to employ people. Seán Quinn lost millions, maybe billions, on gambling. What seemed to have been his real downfall was buying and selling shares or maybe buying and not selling shares when you should. Most people in the media who never traded in stocks and shares will class this as 'greed'. Maybe it is in part 'greed'.

My old buddy Warren Buffett's famous phrase is, 'Be greedy when the rest are fearful and be fearful when the rest are greedy'. This is probably the best advice to get but the most difficult to practice. Maybe it's more appropriate to say, try to be greedy when the rest are fearful and try not to be fearful when the rest are greedy. If we all did things that you should have done in hindsight you would have a lot of millionaires around and everyone on the stock market would be making tons of money. It doesn't work like that. A good job it doesn't as it would have taken a lot of the excitement out of buying and selling shares.

A lot of things in life and business hinge on luck and timing. You can create a lot of your own luck, but it can often be difficult to get the timing right. In 2016 I bought €3,000 worth of shares in GameStop. I had this gut feeling they were going somewhere. They were. Within two years my €3,000 worth of shares in GameStop had dropped to €450. I wasn't a happy camper or a happy investor. I abandoned them out of my head as another bit of bad investing. Then luck struck. In one day my €450 worth of shares in GameStop rocketed to €6,000. I put in to sell. They sold out at a total of €5,800, up from €450 two days previous. What I didn't know was that Ga-meStop shares were set to rocket in price. So much so that the shares I sold for €5,800 on a Friday morning would have rocketed further in the next two working days. Instead of selling at a good profit after a few bad years, after the two days after the weekend I could have sold for €65,000.

People said to me, 'You must be sick as a parrot'.

'No,' I said, 'because three weeks before I was within two inches of winning six million in the lotto because I marked in number eight instead of number twelve' which are less than a half inch away from one another. Similarly, I marked six instead of two. So, I ended up with just one of the lotto numbers even though it was a very close call. Why did I do this and all the numbers there in a two inch square. So near and yet so far. That's how life can pan out.

If hindsight was the future, I would be a millionaire several times over and so would many more. That's why it's best to live for the future because there is no future or millions in the past, only the ones you have passed.

Today I don't get too bogged down in what I lose or what I make in life. It's more important to be happy in what you do instead of trying to convince yourself that everyone else has a great life and I'm the slave who has to keep people enjoying the good life in the life they have become accustomed to. These people may have the same thoughts as me, about me.

If that's the way you feel, spare a thought for Sam Bankman-Fried who brought FTX into a $32 billion company with a few of his friends in a basement flat in America and within ten months his company was worth 0 (nothing) with debts running into bil-lions. The only downside to that is the 30 year old can't enjoy his $32 billion which if it worked out, he could have access to in later life. For him it was only about wealth, ego and independence on fictitious paper, a bit like my Leaving Cert results. Good to look at and reminisce about.

Chapter 49

The life of billionaires

London is the home to many billionaires, and it is classed as the billionaire's capital of the world. It's nothing unusual for an Indian billionaire to spend £30 million on a home in London. I lived there myself one time. I got out of the place because of the rough element. Someone stole my Ferrari from outside my pad one night, the next night they came back and stole my Rolls Royce. I had enough of it, so I bailed out to Castlebar. It's important for millionaires and billionaires to have property in and around London. There are over 100 billionaires who now own property in London.

An Indian billionaire spent over £1 billion on homes in London in one year. He doesn't live in any of them. One of them he has never slept in despite the fact that the butlers change the beds every day, put pots of fresh flowers in vases every day while a host of butlers look after the gardens, presumably watering the flowers, cabbage, carrots and lettuce for the slugs to eat. Most of the high priced properties were not around 15 years ago. One twenty five million mega mansion in North London has a fully fitted out gym with two swimming pools on the top floor. One pool for each of their two children off their bedrooms.

Growing up in Leitrim some years ago, we had a swimming pool on our property which I loved plunging into on a sunny summer's day. It was filled naturally by rainwater. The pool had a soft bottom which I was told the black like substance was very good for your complexion and good looks. That's why I ploughed and swam through it every sunny day. It was known in Leitrim as a bog hole.

Back in London they were importing Irish bog soil to use in the mud baths of London. All for the same purpose as I did. Some of this precious soil was used in one private London property to build a nine hole golf course. The home which was 20,000 sq. ft had everything. You could swing a cat in it, you could swing an elephant in most of the rooms. The whole set up was a bit like present day

Ireland where everyone now wants their friends to come and visit their new bar, their new cinema or play a game of snooker in their games room. Snakes and ladders and twenty five, are but a distant memory for the wealthy billionaires.

They even fitted large screens in their bathrooms so you can watch Fr Ted when you're on the throne or lying in the bath. The whole idea of owning a pad like this in London or New York, is like one up man ship. The word may go out that Oliver Kelleher bought Wickham Lodge in Highgate for £30 million. I certainly would feel important if this spin went out about me. I lived in many areas around London but not in or around Highgate or Grosvenor Sq. These places didn't really appeal to me. There were too many toffs who wouldn't speak to me on the street. These high end properties were valued at around £20 million when I was there. They are now selling at up to £100 million. The main reason people buy these expensive properties for millions is to keep out poor people and riffraff like me which I think isn't fair.

One little house I looked at had a price of £95 million. It was 33,000 sq. ft. It didn't appeal to me. The swimming pool was Olympic size with an island in the middle of it. You got to the island by an automatic drawbridge where you drank foreign liqueurs or your favourite champagne. A robot tractor mowed the lawns, a bit of a waste or you could get the ten acre garden with a John Deere mower and save the bales.

Monaco is the second smallest country in the world after the Vatican. In Monte Carlo you could pick up a nice three bedroom apartment with a view of the sea, sky and more tower blocks for about €40 million. I have to say the view was something else for someone with a few bob. Down in the harbour you could berth your 200 ft yacht. For me that's too big. I would prefer to have something around 100 ft for easy handling and docking. The big problem with these 'properties' is they cannot continue to keep building upwards, so they are now going down three or four storeys for the pool or the gym. This could put a few million pounds onto your street level property.

Many of the billionaires who buy or build multimillion-euro homes that they may never live in, are on an ego trip to be one step ahead of their billionaire neighbour. Some go so far as to replica their 'home' to resemble a five star hotel in their neighbourhood. They may have hundreds of objections to their plans, but they are seldom refused planning permission. Most of the outsides of these London homes have remained unchanged as many are listed buildings but inside some owners may add four more storeys underground.

My old buddy Warren Buffet, who is the third richest person in the world at about $70 billion, has one home. The home he has lived in since the sixties. His reason for only having one home is a simple formula, 'I can only live in one home at any time', he told me. I somewhat agreed with his philosophy. Buffet prefers to buy trains and railroads or planes and runways to land his plane. He used to ride a bike when he was a young fella of 80. For most of these highflyers I have come across, very few of them go out to buy a home. Most of them go out to buy a property they can acquire so they can add another jewel to their property portfolio. Whether they enjoy buying these I don't know, but they certainly enjoy keeping up with the Jones or one step ahead of the Jones more than anything else in life.

I'm on my way to Monaco now just to see how my friends operate there. It's the richest area in the world where a four bed apartment overlooking the sea can cost you up to £60 million, £30 million for the apartment and £30 million for the view. The place has over 2,000 millionaires and even 60 billionaires. That's in a country of a few square miles and a population of 35,000 people. In the middle of Monaco is Monte Carlo. This is the home of five star hotels and casinos where my friends were spending their hard earned money. In Monaco they pay little or no taxes so you can understand why these people come to live there.

Outside the five star hotel, De Paris, there were six Bentley's, five Rolls Royce's, a few Lamborghini's, Ferrari's and a Morris Minor. Anything that money can buy, Monaco can deliver it. One highflier I met was interested in buying a super jet for himself and the family with seating for over forty guests, a gym, swimming pool, a fully fitted bar and restaurant and chefs on hand. The buyer asked what it would cost with all the extras. When told the cost of $300 million, he scratched his head and made the comment, 'I would need to sell a lot of oil to pay that kind of money'. Deal done.

Some of my buddies in Monaco tell me I could live a pretty comfortable life there with about £10 million. The fact you don't pay tax there means I would need about £25 billion back in Ireland to live the same lifestyle and no guarantee of sun. I'm on the way home and sort of decided I'll hold onto my money just in case another new coalition comes into power and slaps an 80 or 90 percent tax on my money and I'd end up back where I started in the middle of another recession.

Over the past 50 years, there have been more billionaires surfacing around the world than ever before in our history. At one time most of the billionaires made their fortune in oil, property or commodities like coal, steel and all those precious metals that lie under the seas or under the earth. More people became millionaires of late from all the new technology like the internet and social media and gadgets that make life a bit simpler for all of us. There are yokes and gadgets we can no longer live without. None of us can live without a mobile phone. When they pack up, like mine did last week, I felt I was lost in this big crazy world where I could phone no one nor did I know who was ringing as I lost all my numbers.

Was it the end of the world? It was but I didn't panic because panicking won't fix my phone. Three days and friends I met were saying 'you don't answer your phone'. Years ago, if you didn't answer your phone, you weren't at home so they could ring you back when you were at home. Nowadays, you can't do that because you don't know when the person will be at home. How did we manage in the past with no phone? You wrote a letter or called around to your friend's house. That day is gone. How would we survive if we had to return to that? Badly and it would probably be the biggest upset in our life that a lot of people would not be able to cope with. I don't want to think of it.

Chapter 50

Switzerland

L ast month I went on a fact finding mission to a small country that is part of Europe but not part of the EU. We often wonder here in Ireland how any country in Europe but not in the EU can survive.

Switzerland is a country half the size of Ireland with eight million people. Over half the country is mountainous which can cause many problems with regard to transport and building of infrastructures. Despite this it is one of the most developed countries in the world. Zurich and Geneva have each been ranked among the top cities in the world in terms of quality of life. It is also ranked near the top globally in several metrics of national performance and government transparency. Have we anything to learn from them? We have, but the people who should learn from them have no interest in learning from them.

On my visit I was very impressed with their common sense approach to everything. They are not too worried about Brexit, Swisexit, Francexit or any other exit. They do their own thing in their own way that suits the people of Switzerland. They know how to run their affairs and survive financially without any EU grants or handouts.

They use a practical approach to everything, including food regulations and Health & Safety regulations. Despite the fact you seldom see police or police vehicles on the roads or in the towns one feels safe everywhere. I stayed with a friend high up in the mountains overlooking Geneva with over 200 houses built in clusters. Security, break ins or robberies are not a regular talking point like they are in Ireland. Every day when we travelled out across the border into France or down the mountain into Geneva we never locked the door of the car or the house. One would imagine by Irish standards this would be impossible as the area I stayed in for the week was only four kilometres from the French border with easy access to hop over and back at will.

Switzerland is a famous food producing country. It is the home to some of the largest food companies in the world. One of these companies, Nestlé, employs over 333,000 people worldwide, producing everything from coffee to biscuits to chocolate. It's not unusual to see a farmer on the outskirts of Geneva with 25 acres employing ten people producing their own country butter, cheeses, honey, fruit and vegetables. Every yard of accessible space is used to produce something that people eat and use. They produce fabulous breads, wines and apples, with vines growing on flat rocks on the sides of mountains where they have to import the clay to make up the ground. Pollution is not evident anywhere.

Lake Geneva which is 580 square kilometres and 73 km long is a hive of activity with lakeside restaurants, canoeing, fishing, pleasure boats, man-made beaches with imported sand and a host of other activities. Over 10,000 people are employed in these lakeside activities.

All along the lakes birds and wildlife mingle with human life. The local authorities and the do-gooder organisations take a different view to conservation and preservation than we do here in Ireland.

The Swiss approach is if you put wildlife habitats out of human sight, the wildlife can easily be wiped out. For that reason and many more wildlife like to mingle with humans because they are protected and get regular feeding from the many tourists who appreciate wildlife and its protection.

Part of these facilities along Lake Geneva could easily be replicated in places like Lough Lannagh in Castlebar town where all the facilities are there on a smaller scale. Unfortunately, we don't act or see the opportunities the Swiss see even at a time when opportunities that can create a lot of business with very little cost are staring us in the face.

Why do our politicians and planners together with Fáilte Ireland and Ireland West personnel not look at how things operate successfully in Switzerland and other countries? We have been spoiled by Europe. We have been cripples with daft regulations and we find it difficult to see the wood from the trees.

Talking of wood, the Swiss cut down over €3 billion worth of timber every year for firewood and house building. Timber is a huge earner so much so that every tree that's cut down is replaced immediately by five trees for future generations.

The whole process and ways of doing business in this small highly populated country shows that a lot of people who run the country get a lot of things right. Their compo culture is non-existent because the rules are that you are 50 percent responsible for your own action. So, if you bang your knee on a table in a restaurant and expect to get €20,000 in compo you will be told by a judge (if it ever goes to court) that you have to look out for legs on tables and not hit them with your knee, toe or head. For most people who live here as in many other countries in the world one has to watch what they are about so they don't get injured. Unfortunately, or fortunately there is no soft money to be made from claiming. Free legal aid is not permitted and all claims are contested by the person who is being sued.

For those of you who may be thinking of moving to Switzerland to live off the state, sue the state and use the taxpayers as fodder you better think again. To gain entry you need to have a job that can sustain your lifestyle in one of the most expensive countries in the world. You may, if you qualify for residency, have to wait up to seven years before you get the go ahead.

The best approach if you're desperate might be to live in the border town of Divonne in France and hop over the border into Crassier in Switzerland to work. Your home in France could cost you half the price it cost one mile across the border in Switzerland and the cost of living could be half the price. It's worth thinking about it if you want to be part of one of the best run countries in the world.

Switzerland is unique in the fact that it has never been bombed or attacked in the past 200 years. The main reason for this is the fact that Hitler and his crew stock filled all their looted gold and wealth in Swiss banks so it wasn't 'rocket science', you don't destroy your own wealth. Nowadays Swiss banks hold trillions of dollars and other currencies from wealthy individuals from all over the world. I still believe they still hold on to confidentiality agreements with their wealthy clients where they don't make information available to tax authorities in other countries. I haven't tested things out on that as it doesn't bother me despite the fact that I own a few shares in Nestlé which pay me 8 times the amount in dividends that Irish banks pay in interest on deposits.

Switzerland never has a housing crisis because they address issues before they become problems. One off houses are rarely built nowadays. Clusters of twelve houses and twelve family apartments are the norm in the mountainous areas. It means one roadway, one sewage pipe, one electricity supply line to the cluster of houses and apartments. It creates a nice, friendly and safe atmosphere in an area that would otherwise be a bleak, mountainous space.

On my way up the mountain by tram we pass or stop at various points along the way and at one stage ten miles into the mountain I disembark at La Jay Clinique. When you step out of the tram there is one lift to take you up to the reception area of the hospital, another lift takes you to the A&E with the same thing replicated on the opposite track going down the mountain. The hospital was busy but well organised with the average appointment on time.

Health insurance here is expensive. More than double the price of Ireland. Many people here would class it as a 'rip off' and bad value for money. Then you have to take stock and evaluate what's good value or bad value for money. My view would be if you pay any price for a service that is not there its bad value for money. If you pay big money for a good service like they have in Switzerland, it's good value for money because you know what you are getting for your money.

On a day trip to Vevey I visited the country market where 500 people were employed selling fish, cheese, local wines and apple juice. I downed 12 scrumptious oysters that tasted like nothing I ever had before. I could have downed a variety of homemade sausage and cooked free range chickens that were displayed in the open on tables. Regularly I stop in shock and think these people wouldn't be allowed to sell their wares in this fashion in Ireland. At 2pm the stall holders dismantled their units, packing sides of Parma ham, cheeses, jams and juices into their vehicles. The council workers are on hand to sweep up and hose down the marketplace to have it ready for the next event.

I'm still bamboozled and cannot understand how regulations can vary so much from one European country to another and why we don't model any of our survival plans on the Swiss plan.

Chapter 51

Setting sail for America

My mother used to tell me I couldn't settle anywhere, I was always 'cocked' for going. To me everything was a challenge I wanted to be part of. I got what I thought was the chance of a lifetime to sail to America with Jarlath Cunnane and his crew of six. I looked at myself as a good sport who was prepared to try anything exciting.

So, for sailing to America, Jarlath built his boat in his own back yard, another challenge. If Christopher Columbus did it, why not me? I had never sailed more than three miles past Westport before this. I wasn't prepared even though I was being accompanied on the two week journey by five more experienced mariners.

We left Westport harbour on a sunny Monday evening and headed for America. The first leg of a journey that would bring us to the Azores, then onto Halifax, up to Newfoundland and back to Westport on a journey that would take six weeks. Sailing can be a brilliant sport. Any sport can be a brilliant sport if you know the ropes and have the skills and the interest in doing them. Sailing is a bit different. When you are 600 miles out in the ocean in a boat that's hopping around in the water surrounded by sharks, it's not the best experience. You couldn't decide 'I have enough of this. Get me out of here'. You're grounded or watered with no turning back.

The nights were long and dark, while I sat up 'on watch' at four in the morning. Our biggest threat was if I fell asleep, that a huge container ship with a load of bananas on its way to Canada could mistake us for a white swan in the distance. Neither did I want to be upended by a cargo ship carrying spare parts for Fiat cars to Montreal.

These were the only two signs of life we saw on the seas for ten days. The only way we knew we were heading for America was watching the planes flying overhead on the way to New York or Boston. I was never groomed for high winds. Maybe the wind blowing the top off a cock of hay on our hill meadow in Leitrim.

One storm blew us 140 miles off course after our back-up engine failed. Up to then we were depending on the sails. Depending on sails in high wind can be a disaster. You can be blown all over the place with no footpaths or ditches to stop you. Wet, worn and weary we spotted the coast of the Azores. We landed and staggered our way up the pier and into Peter's Bar. It's the 'Inn' place to head for to rest the weary bones for the rest of the journey. At that point I decided I'll leave it to Christopher Columbus and Jarlath Cunnane to discover the rest of the world.

After two weeks of adventure, disastrous aching bones and a pain in my head from all the wind and rain that blew through it, I decided I had enough. I got the next flight back to Portugal and back to normal life with my head reeling from all the rocking and rolling on the waves in the Atlantic for nearly two weeks. It wasn't my scene. It's not everyone's scene even though it is one of the most popular sports in the world for the rich and famous.

America is known as the promised land. For many Irish people it was more than the promised land. I was always told that Bethlehem or Jerusalem was the promised land because that's where our lord was born and reared.

For over two centuries Irish people took the boat to America. It wasn't too far away. You could nearly see it from Belmullet. We were lucky. It was a first resort and a last resort for many. There was wealth and prosperity there when there was starvation and hunger here. We had a famine that destroyed many people's lives. Even in today's world when we are supposed to have everything, there are families in some parts of the world starving, yet we dump out so much food that would easily feed all the millions of people who die from famine.

Travelling to America was always our dream or else the relatives coming home from America. We didn't have any near relations in America, so I never saw a dollar until I was 16. It didn't bother me. The fella's photo that was on the dollar had a very dour looking face. It wouldn't tempt you to go to America, but I did.

Chapter 52

My colourful relations in America – Chicago May

My mother was a great woman to follow the family tree. She had records of our relations going back nearly 200 years. My brother Aiden took after her because he has continued the family tree and put most of it into print and video.

Some people don't know who their relations are. They say the only relative you can be sure of in life is your mother. Relatives in today's world may be people you never met because there are so many Irish people scattered all over the world who you may never have seen only on Facebook or Twitter. In the past you might not have seen them unless you got a photo from America or England. Big families in the past didn't all stay around home. Once they left school, they went to either England or America.

We had relations where there were 23 in the family, 12 brothers and 11 sisters. Their father was a farmer and their mother a housewife. The youngest in the family was a boy. He never saw six of his sisters because they had gone to America before he was born. Tough times, happy times, hard times, made up of sadness, love and joy. There were many American 'wakes' when 15 of a family were emigrating. They say history repeats itself in many ways.

Today people are emigrating and migrating in every part of the world. For the Irish they emigrated because of hunger, adventure, excitement and the chance to better themselves. Many of them made it big in many parts of the world. They were given the opportunities to work and earn money and give something back to keep the country they settled in viable. If you didn't get these opportunities, you ended up homeless on the streets of New York or the streets of London. Many Irish made it 'big' abroad in many walks of life in politics, construction, hospitality and criminality.

America was a hotbed for criminality in the last century. There was no law or order in some areas. It was an era where gangland figures and bank robbers had more access to guns than the police had. It's a bit like that here in Ireland.

There is a story told about an Irish garda who stopped a van on a quiet country road in the west of Ireland. It had two male occupants. The garda asked the driver to see his credentials, ie his drivers' licence. The driver reached down and picked up a gun from the ground and pointed it at the garda. His options were limited on a quiet country road, so he stepped aside and let the van and occupants proceed on their journey. Later, when he was giving his report on the matter to his local superintendent, he said he asked the driver to show him his driver's licence and the driver pulled a gun on him.

The garda chief asked, 'and what did you do then?'

'What would you do?' replied the garda, 'if you were standing there with someone pointing a loaded gun at you and you there pointing the butt of a leaded pencil at him.'

Enough said, no further questions. My theory that a butt of a pencil is worth all the brains in the world doesn't stand up after you hear about these things really happening.

Despite that, I still believe you can work out many mathematical problems faster with the butt of a pencil than you can with most of the fancy apps and technology we have today. When things don't work as they should, millions or billions of euros or dollars could be wiped off the value of any business. All you have to do is look at the collapse of the crypto company, FTX. They went from being worth $32 billion in the beginning of 2022 to zero in the space of ten months. Obviously, nobody knows who hit the wrong button. Unlike the butt of a pencil, nobody recognises their writing which we could all do in the past to find out who did what because it was there in black and white.

Chicago was the hotbed for many Irish. One distant relative of mine made it her home for a couple of decades in the 1900s until her death in 1929.

My relation, May Duignan was born in the parish of Killoe in Co Longford. You could see the parish from Odie's room window across the border from Leitrim. We could see more of Co Longford from that window than you could of Co Leitrim. My grandmother was Mary Rose Duignan before she married, and I was told she was a second cousin of May Duignan's mother. We had and still have close relations named Duignans on my father's side of the family. Tommy Joe Duignan was married to my aunt Mary who was my father's sister. We had relations in Cloone, called Kellehers, who we were related to us on my mother's side. We were a kind of a 'mixed up lot' in many ways.

Mary Annie Duignan was born on St Stephen's Day in 1871. She was destined for the bright lights of Chicago. At the age of 19, May, as she was known as, sold four of her mother and father's cattle at a fair in Longford and ran away to Liverpool with the money. She then got a boat to America and then onto Nebraska to stay with her uncle.

May soon married her American lover Dal Churchill. The marriage didn't last long as he got lynched in a botched train robbery and died. Their marriage gave May American citizenship. She then moved to Chicago where she became a career criminal pick-pocketing and robbing drug stores and eventually she got a five year term in prison for her crimes. After being released and having made good contacts in prison, she joined the criminal underworld, got involved in all sorts of gangsterism including assaults, robberies, brawling and drunk and disorderly behaviour. She changed her name and features a number of times to avoid detection by the police.

Later on, in her career she met Eddie Guerin, a major criminal who organised robberies across America and Europe. May and Eddie sailed to Europe to organise a robbery at the American Express office in Paris. She was arrested and sentenced with Guerin to 15 years in jail. Both were imprisoned on a French prison island where Guerin escaped and made his way back to London.

In 1907 after May was released, she took up with another gangster named Charley Smith. After an altercation Guerin shot Smith in the foot. Both Guerin and May were jailed for another term for attempted murder in London. On their release, May returned to the US.

At this time May was one of the most wanted women in America. Like the Bonnie and Clyde characters at the time, they were almost untouchable. They were armed with submachine guns at a time the authorities hadn't the money to fit the police out with handguns.

By the 1920s May Duignan had hit hard times. She was abandoned in Detroit and had become destitute. She hoped to make money by approaching print houses to publish her memoirs. Her book Chicago May, The Queen of Crooks was published in 1928. Her former lover Eddie Guerin published his life story at the same time titled, 'I was a Bandit'. May Duignan, Chicago May, The Queen of Crooks died in 1929 at the age of 59.

During those years Chicago was the home to many people who emigrated from Mayo and Longford. Most of the Leitrim people who emigrated ended up in New York. They used to say it was the handiest place to go as it was on the corner as you go into America. On my first visit to New York, I was brought up to date on many of the gangsters who ruled the city.

The relation who I stayed with at the time would have known or known of most of them as they were in the bar and hospitality business. Most of the gangsters made their money offering protection for a percentage of the takings. At that time in Ireland the Civil War was in full flight so many left Ireland or were told to leave or get shot. America at the time was ruled by gangsters and Ireland was in a similar situation where people were being shot in every parish in Ireland. Your chances of succeeding as a gangster in America were better. You were unknown to other people in your neighbourhood. Unlike at home, it was a lot harder to be recognised.

One family I know had four of their relatives emigrate or were forced to emigrate during our Civil War. They spent 15 years of their young lives in New York working for the mafia as enforcers. After 15 years they returned to Ireland and bought up all around them and lived a normal life here until they died.

Everyone knew their pedigree and their background but nobody raised the issue. Nobody could because their own families might have taken part in atrocities during the Civil War. We Irish were the greatest fighters in the world. We spent 800 years trying to get the Brits out of Ireland. We still haven't got them out. Other countries where British rule was in for much fewer years had more luck.

In many of these places, the British left voluntarily. With all the hassle we gave them, you would imagine they would be only too happy to get out fast.

Was it the oil and gas we have around our coast? Is it the fact we are their only real neighbours left in Europe? Was it the millions of tons of fish we have in the waters around us that are being robbed from us? Anything is possible in love and war.

Chapter 53

Experts in every field

Ireland has become a nation inhabited by experts, opinionists, whingers and know all's who have a view on everything, even things they know nothing about. We have become obsessed with money, lack of money and spending money especially when it's not our own. We fight and argue about what is value for money, the projects we spend it on, and we are obsessed with people and the way they behave. We are obsessed with events and how they may or may not pan out. We are obsessed with Brexit and how it may or may not pan out for us. We were and still are obsessed with Donald Trump's way of doing business and the way he planned to build a wall around Mexico. We are obsessed with the way the Irish government plans to build a hospital in Dublin.

The border in this country is not that unlike the US/Mexican border. There will always be a certain amount of smuggling and looking for value.

I did the same type of smuggling when I was a young fella in Leitrim. The opportunity was there, the border wall only a few miles down the road so you couldn't let a good deal pass when it meant you could put cheap bread and butter on the table and cheap petrol in the car.

I'm nearly radicalised myself at this stage continuously listening to all the things that the experts say. When you hear the 'experts' you're nearly inclined to believe them and their reports. These 'experts' are making a load of money for some government agency who asks them to conduct surveys so they can then create new rules and regulations that will make another load of dosh for another new agency to write more regulations and warnings on the things that are bad for us. I see another new expert group have come up with a new set of warnings that could kill us all if we don't watch ourselves. I have read what the 'experts' have proposed in their plan to print health warnings on gin, Irish gin only.

I'm now going to tell you for free the things in life you should never do if you don't want to go deaf, blind, get a heart attack, die of cancer or fall asleep when you are in the swimming pool. My first public warning, and I think it should be printed in big print on all packets of cotton buds is you can go deaf if you stick cotton buds into your ear. If you decide to leave them in both ears you will go deaf instantly. Warning number two, I used to hear some years ago that you will go blind from too much sexual activity. If you put yourself in a stressful situation, like someone opening a window in the bedroom and they come in at 4 o'clock in the morning and frighten the daylights out of you even though they come in the window at night. This can cause a heart attack. So, my advice is don't sleep in the bed beside the window.

There is another thing we all have problems with and that's sleeping or trying to sleep because all sorts of bad thoughts may be going through your mind. This can cause you to be drowsy and unable to drive safely to work the next day if you don't get enough sleep. So, I suggest in this case you jump out of the bed, turn on the radio and listen to Midwest Radio. If you need sleep during the day, take a few hours off so you can lie around bull dozing which you are probably doing anyway whether you had a good night's sleep or not.

Another survey I conducted is that a written warning should be sent to everyone not to indulge in counting sheep. Experts tell me the best way to fall asleep is to start counting sheep. So, my advice to you is not to start counting sheep as you drive through Partry and Tourmakeady as it can be damaging to your health and counting sheep can make you drowsy. Another printed warning I plan to have on all Irish bulls and rams will be that a bull and a ram can kill you if you try to attack or rob their young or any of their family. The same warning, I plan to print on bees and wasps nests if you decide to attack them. I got a rude awakening from 5,000 wasps one time when I decided to act the brave man and shift them out of their house in a cow shed.

In the meantime, I think you have enough food for thought here. It's my way of joining the rest of the 'experts' in advising you how to live a healthy, happy and stress-free life and remember to always read the labels and if you happen to be drinking Gunpowder Gin in New York check the warning label on the bottle that it could cause you cancer. There won't be a label on the bottle, but if you drink the gin in Leitrim or Mayo there will be a label warning you. So now you may understand how I decided to become an 'expert' on the art of living and dying, just read the instructions because it's only a gin thing and it won't happen in America.

Chapter 54

Robots

Over the next 20 years many experts claim that many of our existing businesses, trades and services will disappear or close down as a result of new technology. Look at how products were manufactured 100 years ago. Henry Ford started producing cars in America and at the time of full production they had more than 65 plants worldwide and employed over 175,000 staff working on assembly lines, bolting on panels, spraying the shell of the car, polishing it and getting it ready for the market. In the past twenty years most of the workers have been replaced by robots. These were the first signs that the world of mass production of products was going down the road. Obviously, every other business operator looked at the new methods of mass production without people having to do the work. This cut down dramatically on labour costs, insurance costs and waste. Today in Ireland most of our metal manufacturing companies are gone out of business because they couldn't afford to fit robots to manufacture products we were producing in small lots. The Chinese and the Germans could produce a cheap product using lighter materials that robots could weld. They weren't the same product but the price difference meant they looked much better value for money. So that put paid to a top-class product that might last for years that nobody wanted to last for years.

Since then we see other trades that will not last the pace. How should we plan for this? Ensure we have less people in the world or create more sustainable jobs to replace them. Am I being a pessimist in predicting the demise of some of the things in life and the jobs for life we could never imagine might disappear? This is my call and I'm not saying it will happen, might happen or could happen.

To put my thoughts in the picture for you I will outline the trades I feel will bite the dust and the reasons why. Drivers of buses, trains and lorries will be replaced with self-drive electric vehicles that won't need drivers but will be controlled by a person sitting at a computer and pressing buttons. Next, we will see the demise of printers, publishers of books, magazines and newspapers. All of these will be available on your smartphone or laptop. ATM machines will disappear as will high street banks because paper money will be replaced by plastic and the high streets are dying a death already. Farmers will become an endangered species because of regulations from the EU and the fact that the old ways of farming with a shovel and grape will be replaced by an electric powered machine controlled from a central depot probably in your local co-op.

The cashier in your local supermarket or takeaway will disappear to be replaced by a scanner that will tell you what to do and say, 'Thank you, hope you have a nice day', even though they don't see you or care too much about you. Travel agents will disappear to be replaced by online bookings or booking agents in India or Bangalore. Factory workers will be replaced by robots who only stop working when they need to be serviced. Warehouse staff will get their marching orders as they will be replaced in warehouses by 'pickers'. These are the yokes that operate in Amazon and most online businesses. They simply read your order and pick it off the shelf, label it and move it onto the conveyer belt to be wrapped and dispatched to the customer in America or Russia. Recently Walmart introduced 1500 robots to their stores, to mop floors, load and unload lorries and pick orders off shelves for customers who order online. Bartenders and restaurant workers will be in the firing line too. Again, there will be an app on the bar or restaurant counter to order your drinks and meals and a robot in the kitchen will cook it, put it on a conveyer belt and land it on the table in front of you. If you have a complaint you have two options, shut up or eat up. Computers don't talk back or listen to complaints.

Most people behind a counter will disappear as is already happening in many banks and other government departments that you are no longer able to talk to on the phone. You will be simply told 'email your query'. Within hours or minutes, you may get an email back telling you they have your email and that's the last you may ever hear from them. Obviously, if it's the revenue commissioners you are dealing with you will hear back from them.

The other trade that will bite the dust are construction workers. Their shovel and spade will be replaced by an earth moving machine with one big bucket on the front and back. This will be operated by a computer to dig a hole on the side of the road to lay pipes or cables. You may see this in action on many roads with five or six extra workers breastfeeding the shovel while they all look into the same hole. I'm not sure if their jobs will be in jeopardy because of the fact that these types of jobs have been around for a long time and in most cases a computer can't do that sort of work.

The world of telesales people may disappear again to be taken over by voice mailing machines who know your name, phone number and date of birth without ever meeting with you. Gone will be those people who phone you up to tell you that you have just won $10 million in a lotto in Nigeria and they need your banking details so they can lodge the $10 million in your account. I would miss these friendly fellas phoning me, so I hope these aren't obliterated.

Years ago, the shaving razor that would cut the face off you was the only weapon for a person to shave with. Then came the electric razor, simpler, safer and less hassle or mess. We thought it was the end for the old hand razor but no, it has held on and is still the most popular yoke to shave with.

Another area we may see huge changes in is air travel. Many of these are already with us. Military aircrafts can fly to any destination in the world, drop a bomb and kill hundreds of people and return safely back to the air base with nobody at the controls. So, pilots will get their flying notice that they will no longer be needed. The same with soldiers because we will no longer need soldiers to fight wars. The world will no longer need armies, just a robot that doesn't stop half way through the job of work because the battery ran out. So, soldiers will get their marching orders.

I remember before all this technology hit Ireland, CIE brought in the one-man bus (I don't think there were women bus drivers then). One double decker bus ploughed into a lamp post on Henry Street. The driver was questioned and asked why he was not watching where he was going so as to avoid the crash. His answer was simple enough, 'How could I see where I was going, I was upstairs collecting fares when it crashed'. So, in fairness modern technology doesn't always work unless you know, or you are shown how it works and your little brain can withstand the wind of change.

Many family farms and farmers will disappear to be replaced by factory farms or plantations. Bees and honey will probably disappear because of the overuse of pesticides. A lot of humans may disappear because of the overuse of powerful weed killers that are on the market today. Some of these weed killers can kill weeds two feet down in the earth. If it can do that, what does it do to the food we eat that is planted within days of the spraying of the weed killer?

To add to this list, you can include other items that will disappear in the next two decades. Cameras, watches, alarm clocks, petrol cars, travelling shops (are already gone), turf, coal mines and coal miners, radios, tape recorders, churches, priests, stamps, rural garda stations, landline phones, phone boxes, rural post offices, rural pubs, rural towns and if we don't cop ourselves on, rural Ireland could disappear.

The oceans are polluted with mountains of plastic, oil and waste that is killing off our fish stocks. Our land, lakes and rivers are polluted with oceans of plastic and other waste which will eventually wipe us all out. I'm not saying we should get alarmed about this, but we should do something about it. We need to get serious at the top and learn the best way to save the earth.

Why not bring back the ham and bacon slicers we all saw in our local shops a few years ago which are now frowned upon by health inspectors in Ireland? You ordered your ten rashers or six slices of ham. It was sliced fresh for you, placed on greaseproof paper and into a paper bag. That day has gone in Ireland and these healthy options are gone because of daft EU regulations. They have been replaced by plastic trays that are then wrapped in plastic. Every supermarket display fridge is full of this rubbish; we cannot see it as that. The food looks attractive and healthy and that's what matters.

So, where do we start? The first stand should be to educate the regulators and show them where to start and show them where their job should end instead of talking bullshit about issues that they don't know how to handle and control. That's the story of our lives.

Obviously, there is no point in me or anyone else complaining unless we have a plan. So, my suggestion is to take it seriously and get the resources in place, human resources, first to clean up our streets, rivers and land of rubbish that's blowing around. Pay teams of Tidy Town & Country volunteers. Prosecute people who dump illegally. We should get all those people who get community service fines in the court out there to give something back to their community by cleaning up the rubbish they dumped. Chances are that will never happen. It could happen with the stroke of a pen and brains.

Chapter 55

The cost of living and the art of survival

We never stop listening to experts giving us all advice on how to live a healthy life, which is good advice. We have more people trying to get us to eat more rubbish which may lead to an unhealthy life. We have others telling us how to survive on a budget. Turn down the heat and freeze to death. Stop drying your clothes in the dryer, fill your dishwasher before you turn it on. Wrap yourself in a warm Foxford blanket, wear a cap and socks in bed. Don't go to bed on your own. If you don't have a partner, bring the cat, dog or hamster to snuggle up to you and keep you warm. There is no shortage of experts to advise us on everything.

Supermarkets will boast that nobody beats their prices. Very few people will advise you how to turn out a good family meal for ten people on a budget. These things you have to learn yourself by shopping around and working to a budget by buying good, fresh, nourishing, healthy foods that are often better value than most higher class food.

Some good products have rocketed in price while others are still good value for money. Having worked in the supermarket business, it gave me a good head for figures and prices which we all had to remember on the top of our heads instead of getting the answer on an adding machine where the batteries may be dead. It's not a difficult job to remember how to add up. There are only nine numbers you need to remember from 0 to 9. It's pretty simple. They are easy to remember and add up with a butt of a pencil. People can be amazed at people who can add up figures in their heads.

The real experts on these things are dart players and auctioneers. A few years ago, they brought out a wall mounted calculator for scoring at darts which was the opposite to an adding machine.

They were subtracting machines. They never took off. The real dart player still wanted the chalk and chalkboard.

Working out the cost of vital essentials is important and it's more important to be able to spot them if you are working on a strict budget. After you buy the food, the most important thing after that is to know how to cook it, which is very simple, if you know how. Everything in life is simple if you know how to do it or be shown how to do it.

Asking anyone nowadays how to work a yoke like a computer is a minefield and the way you are shown how to do it can be a bigger minefield that can explode in your face, and you are more enlightened before the event than after it.

I wasn't the first to start testing and working on computers. When you are left behind, it can be difficult to get to the top of the class. My biggest problem was trying to convince people how little I knew about computers.

I'm still limited as to how much I can do on a computer or a smartphone. I know enough to get by. I remember when computers came out, I asked a neighbour if he knew much about computers.

'I do,' he said, 'I know enough to keep away from them.'

If you're not computer literate nowadays, people think you have some sort of impediment or you are lacking something or you're not right in the head. You could be all of these and still get by except when you try to get through to some government agency or bank for help and they don't answer the phone. A robot may tell you to 'check our website' or call back when someone might answer the phone. That's when you are glad you didn't do a masters in communications or no communications.

Apparently, many people nowadays feel they can do business with you without having to talk to you. It works sometimes. It looks like a great system when it works and the operator in India looks after things, provided he is not passing the buck to a robot who may not speak English.

I'm back in the kitchen trying to cook up a bit of a storm from a recipe I saw on YouTube. It's not a good idea to have a computer beside the kitchen sink with water splattering on it or the screen covered in flour, bread soda, salt and olive oil. Better to try and remember the recipe in your head or write it down for easy cooking. That's when you realise life can be much simpler sticking to the older ways if you want to cook a good meal or bake a perfect cake.

Amazingly, celebrity chefs seldom tell us the basics that most amateur cooks fail at regularly. How not to burn the food by turning the gas up too high or moving away and forgetting to check until the food is burned, and the food ends up in the dog and the pan ends up in the bin and you end up hungry. It's one of the main reasons so many people stay clear of cooking anything that there is more hassle to them than boiling or frying an egg. Been there, done it all.

Going back to the '60s, boxty was known as a delicacy only in Leitrim and a few other 'civilised' places around Ireland. It was the poor man's breakfast, dinner and tea. It was mainly served plain and simple, with plenty of butter fried on the pan with eggs and bacon. Every woman had her own recipe. Like brown bread, it tasted different in every house.

We went to many houses depending if it was cooked on an open turf fire, a timber fire or on a range. We were the envy of everyone in the school and at home.

Today, boxty and black pudding are on the menus in many restaurants around Ireland. You may find it on menus in Melbourne or New York. You will regularly see it on breakfast menus in restaurants instead of cholesterol boosting, fat-filled hash browns.

Over the past few years, I have tried my skills at an array of boxty dishes like boxty and black pudding roulade, boxty bangers, boxty wan tons, boxty dumplings and boxty omelette, which takes about six minutes to turn out and it tastes great. As a treat I will try a boxty pizza or a boxty wrap filled with shredded chicken, pork or beef.

Most countries in the world have their own potato pancake which is similar in taste and texture as our traditional boxty. In other countries it is known as rosti or fried potato bread or potato cakes. You can have your choice, or you can make any of these with little effort. The main ingredient you need is patience and the head for it and stomach to eat it. The same applies to many food products. Some you need more skills and patience than others. Once you have mastered it, you're almost there. For me the worst part is the washing up. You are better to wash as you go because grated potato left in a bowl will go rock hard overnight.

In Ireland we have a great name for quality food, cooked and uncooked. The pity is we cannot grow more of the food we eat. We can grow any fruit or veg in Ireland except fruit with a skin on it like oranges and bananas. We can live with that because there are a few countries who specialise in these. In the past we were nearly self-sufficient with the range of foods we eat. Things have changed. Some for the better, some for the worse.

The incentives have to start with the government backing entrepreneurs who have the skills to do things to better themselves and help our economy grow. We have many countries we could look to and copy their ideas to ensure we can make our homegrown food and goods freely available in retail outlets or farmers' markets in every town in Ireland. These are the greatest attractions in many towns and cities across the world.

Melbourne has one of these markets which attracts thousands of people every day. They run it out of a once closed down railway yard and an old time market area that is fully covered from the elements. There are hundreds of stalls and permanent units selling goods they might not have an outlet to sell elsewhere.

It's not rocket science to see where the opportunities are. Trading goods is one of the oldest skills in the world. Our forefathers took part in the selling of everything from horses to cattle, to sheep, to foul, to farm produce, clothing and household goods. I was given the opportunity many years ago by my father to rear and sell two calves. It's something we all remember forever. The first few pounds you made is always a pleasant memory. It could be an inspiration to many young people today who would like to better themselves.

We in Ireland may need to change a lot of our culture in government offices and departments. How long that could or might take with red tape is debatable. The important thing is to start, and the second most important thing is to make it work with all the people having an input.

Chapter 56

The Taste of Tiernaur

Agood example of showcasing what we have on our own doorsteps was the Taste of Tiernaur which I attended one year in November.

It was a Festival of Food with a difference. Firstly, November is a bad month to try to shift people out of the house for anything because Christmas is down the road and it's a time that gobbles up a lot of saved money. Secondly, the venue for the was unusual in the sense that it took place in a country bar and restaurant. We all hear the stories that country pubs are bolloxed and the same is often said about rural Ireland. You can look at life and business like that if you're in that frame of mind because of the attitude of some politicians and people who control our lives and the way we run our lives.

The Taste of Tiernaur took place in Nevins Bar and Restaurant in Tiernaur. Many people may not have heard of Tiernaur because it's not a city or a town or a village. There isn't even a crossroads there, but Nevins is there. Tiernaur lies on the main road between Newport and the picturesque seaside village of Mulranny. The area has a lot of business disadvantages because at the back of it lies the Nephin Mountains which is home to about 5,000 sheep who don't frequent bars or restaurants. To the front of Nevins lies the Atlantic Ocean with millions of fish that are taken away in foreign EU trawlers. Again, the fish don't frequent bars or restaurants other than to be served up in the dining room. Again, the fact that Nevins and Tiernaur lies in the next parish to America, you have a sort of a disadvantage when it comes to attracting customers. Not so if you are in the right frame of mind and take the right approach and you are given half a chance.

The Taste of Tiernaur highlighted all the great foods we have in Mayo and in the West. When these are cooked professionally or at home you realise what we have to offer on our doorsteps. The Taste of Tiernaur was held in the function room and bar at the classic venue. The chefs in Nevins cooked the food and the staff displayed and served it. In total there was 20 different local foods served such as lamb and black pudding from Newport, mussels and oysters from across the water in Clew Bay, smoked salmon from the Atlantic Ocean, meat pies, barbeque salmon, pork belly, boxty and chowder, my favourite starter, all made with real, natural and tasty ingredients. The local fruit and vegetables were packed and graded in Castlebar and I have to say the potatoes went down well with shredded beef. The black pudding with a topping of monkfish and red cabbage was something you would rarely get in any Michelin Star restaurant in the world.

I'm pounding along the line with my plate, knife and fork tasting everything. I'm in no hurry, I have four hours to eat and have a complementary Guinness, Rockshore or Grace O'Malley Gin to wash down some great local cuisine. In a way I was used to this in my young days in Leitrim with maybe some truffle and caviar sandwiches thrown in. It was great nourishment when you had to spend a hungry day in the bog. Along the line of food in Tiernaur I was spoiled for choice with pork ribs, spare bacon ribs, chicken and lamb kebabs, cooked to perfection and served professionally. I finished the food line with a sampling of colcannon with tender lamb loin and homemade gravy.

Deserts, deserts, I'm told it's not a good recipe for a buck on twenty tablets a day with high blood pressure, diabetes, high and low cholesterol, stents in his heart, gout and a host of other problems I still haven't yet detected. Despite that I had to try it and give my opinion. I only tried the chocolate cup with cheesecake, the chocolate sponge and the fruit filled pizza which I've never seen or eaten before. When the festival ended that night I, along with 400 more guests, discussed among us how businesses in rural Ireland can survive and promote the great quality products we have on our doorsteps. These products have been around for centuries so there should be no reason why we have to import potatoes from Cyprus, lamb from New Zealand, apples from South Africa, garlic from China or lettuce from Spain. With innovation and support from the government agencies and people within those agencies who are probusiness, we could create thousands of jobs in the food and hospitality business. In fairness, Bord Bia and Tourism Ireland are playing their part. Should we not have another five or six agencies playing their part alongside them? Rural Ireland has many entrepreneurial people like John and Ann Nevin in Tiernaur who employ over 40 people in what would otherwise be a jobs blackspot. Again, I stress we should have the Singapore approach where government agencies are all pro-business with personnel there to advise you on the business opportunities and support that are there to help you start a business, create more business and survive in business and support your local community so it doesn't die.

Chapter 57

Why we should look to our own

For generations, Irish people across the world have started and created huge businesses employing thousands of jobs in many areas. Successful Irish people are huge contributors to the world's economy. Two of these people are Leitrim brothers Ray and Des O'Rourke, who are the biggest private building company in the UK turning over billions every year and employing over 10,000 worldwide.

There was a recent RTÉ television programme about the life and times of one of Ireland's richest people, Seán Quinn. The aftermath of the show created more talk as if the show was about Donald Trump's life in business. It was a sad affair for many people employed by the Quinn organisation, the people of the northwest and a traumatic experience for the Quinn family. Some of the comments by a former political leader didn't help because of his experience of people who live in border areas.

For Quinn, he was crucified for one major mistake he made. He bailed out the Anglo Irish Bank and instead of the bank prospering with a new investment, they went wallop. Any business is easy to start, making it successful is the important thing. That depends on the support and back-up you get and the support and back-up of good staff who have the same interest in the business as you have and the authorities who promote jobs in Ireland.

In America or many other countries, when you fail there is no stigma. The approach often is that people will appreciate you for the success you had and the things you give to society. Quinn and his staff were saviours of a very neglected area for over 40 years. The government and politicians took a different view which is sad in any society because it puts it in the minds of people that people like Quinn are the architects of their own misfortune. The TV documentary was watched by a huge amount of people.

After the show I spoke to a number of people about their call and thinking about the whole scenario. Amazingly, the answers depended a lot on the job the people I spoke to worked at. I was surprised by the answers. People in business had a lot of sympathy for Quinn and his family, while others who worked in government jobs made the comment, 'It was pure greed, he brought it all on himself'.

The way the show was portrayed by RTÉ could be described as a cross between the Irish Civil War and the film The Field. Maybe if it were a Dublin-based businessperson and a country bank that were the main players in this saga, we might have seen a different type of view. Or maybe not. Sadly, when politicians, politics and vulture funds get involved, anything is liable to happen, to be said or not said. That's the gamble you take.

I wondered if Quinn had never started the business with one lorry on a hill full of sand with no grants, would the business still be around today? Built up by someone else with the get up and go of Seán Quinn and his dedicated staff? I doubt it.

Greed plays a big part in all our lives. I was hungry for success, but I always wanted to leave a bit for the next person provided they were interested in challenging people. That can be greed. Call it what you like. I don't know what the opposite of greed is in business. Give the stuff away and go broke and you would still probably be classed as greedy.

When I spoke to a few people along the border and across the border who were described as not normal compared to the rest of the people in Ireland, I got a somewhat different attitude. They had the American style approach where they were proud of Seán Quinn and what he had achieved in a part of Ireland that was neglected by the government agencies. They all agreed he was the best man with the best team to run the business profitably with his team around him. If he were an operator of an American or another Irish company in a different trade, chances are he would still be operating the company. Sometimes in business you can make one mistake and it can ruin you. In other cases, you can make a lot of mistakes and be rewarded. We see it all around us. That can happen in love, war and business.

Quinn made the cardinal sin of taking money out of his insurance business to fund shares he bought in Anglo. Insurance companies often commit a lot of venial sins by agreeing to pay out genuine claims for genuine amounts but when they write the cheque, they may deduct up to 25 or 30 percent and they will give no valid reason to do so. The only reason they practice this is because they get away with it. Regularly the regulators both in Ireland and the UK have 'threatened' to look into these types of illegal acts. Up to now it is all talk. When they do see a blatant case, they may fine the insurance company a couple of million euros without ever checking how much overall they have made from the practice.

In many other businesses if you act and behave like that, you are simply struck off. Instead, some of the insurance companies continue their wayward ways until they get another couple of million in fines which they have already recouped. Insurance can be a peculiar business. The price you pay depends on how lucky you are. If you have a couple of fraudulent claims in the hospitality business that are not properly investigated by the insurance company, your annual cost of insurance may be greater than the profit you can make in the business. If and when these businesses collapse, there are a lot of job losses.

It usually isn't an issue politicians or others take too seriously. If they did these issues would have been sorted years ago. Similarly with banks. If they are regulated the way the rest of us are regulated, they all would not have gone wallop. That's life. We have to live with it or shut up

I wrote before about another great Irish company, Ryanair. They are the role models for affordable air travel in the world. Michael O'Leary runs this business with no grants and little back up support or admiration from many Irish politicians or the government. Politicians as a rule don't like people who sell cheap, affordable services. They take a different view to supermarkets and food discounts because that gets votes when they shout about why supermarkets and other businesses should drop their prices, insurance companies and energy companies excluded.

The Michael O'Learys and Seán Quinns of the business world were the people who got our country up and running before the government brought in American vulture funds to mop up many good businesses that Irish people didn't often get the chance to

even bid for. Imagine if Michael Collins or Éamon de Valera went
down the same route and sold Ireland out to foreign vulture funds,
what would our reaction be?

Some people in government and in government agencies like to
run with the hare and hunt with the hound. Is it greed, tactics or
just their entrepreneurial skills? Sadly, when you put stumbling
blocks in the way of enterprising people, it can come back to haunt
you. We sometimes have to have the view that we are doing a good
deed for the country and our economy by giving good assets away
to faceless vulture funds or individuals. We sometimes treat famous people who may have achieved very little only being famous
as iconic people who are our salvation. We saw many of these in
the banking and building world over a decade or more ago.

In September 2023, Miriam O'Callaghan interviewed Seán
Quinn about his involvement in the Anglo shares saga and his new
book where he outlined the facts and set the record straight. He
admitted that he was greedy not for money but to succeed in business. He stated he was one of the lowest paid directors of his company. He had started the business on his farm in Derrylin with few
handouts. He went on to employ thousands of people in a part of
Ireland that was more or less forgotten about by politicians. It was
classed as bandit country. If you were from these parts you had to
fight your own battles and dig your own drains. The attitude by
some politicians and the media was, at the time, and still is, if you
don't operate out of Dublin, you're not in touch with what's happening around Ireland.

That's not always the case. Quinn admitted he made mistakes,
which we all do. There were others who made more serious mistakes and hoodwinked a lot of people into investing in what were
to become disasters, but they ran for cover. Quinn, his family and
a great business paid the price. Today people will say we are all
paying the price.

The biggest price we are paying and generations from now will
have to pay is the billions all the Irish banks gambled. All our
money with the backing of politicians and regulators.

That's a reality we forget when we want to find scapegoats which
politicians and the media are good at finding.

We all can be greedy when it comes to business. You have to be because you have commitments to your family, your staff and your suppliers. There are three main types of greedy people we all meet up with. Some are greedy for money. Others are greedy for power and status. Others are greedy to make a success out of their ambitions and skills.

The first two groups can be hard to handle because they become obsessed with money and power. I often refer to these people as the 3Bs (bigheaded, boring bollixes). They usually have nothing much to talk about except what money they have or what property they own. Seán Quinn took a lot of gambles to build his business and most people in the border counties and around Ireland appreciated what he achieved for his thousands of workers. For others, they want to believe what some politicians, some sections of the media and bankers say and do.

We all have to take gambles in life. When everything does not work out, you should not be nailed to the cross because of one mistake you made. Hopefully we won't stop unstoppable people like Seán Quinn from doing a good job for the Irish people and pay billions in taxes to keep our little country prosperous.

Any business is a challenge. Big businesses or small businesses. If you run a small business, you may find it difficult to get finance to run your business. If you run a big business, you may get too much money from banks that you may not be able even to pay back the interest. I was never in that situation. We ran a tight ship and the time I could have spent juggling finances, I spent looking after my customers and my workers, family and friends. It's a good recipe for peace of mind, it may not be a recipe to become a millionaire or billionaire with other people's money. Then again who wants to be a millionaire.

Whether you are in business or in a full-time pensionable job, you will have to cope with taxes, charges and inflation. If it means you are paying three times the price for a gallon of diesel in Ireland against the US is immaterial. Inflation is here to stay, and business will have to adjust to these changes. Overall prices may drop 1 or 2 percent which means very little when inflation has gone up by 11 percent. It's a pittance of savings. The only way to combat these increases is by the way we all spend our money or waste our money. The person who planned to build a six bedroom house for a family of four may have to resort to a five bedroom house and be happy there, regardless of the size or value of your home. It may be of value to you if you decide to sell the house and live in a caravan and pocket the money. We have many choices we can make in life, but they should be sensible choices.

Running a business is like letting your emotions overrule your brain. We all have dreams and aspirations. Some we can achieve with little effort. Others you can achieve by being ambitious and others you can achieve by being greedy and ruthless with little regard for leaving a bit for the next person. This may make you wealthy, greedy and ignored by a lot of ordinary decent people in business, in family or normal living and working in any job.

We all have the choice in life what to be remembered for when we die. It may or may not be about the money you made or who you left it to. It may be about what sort of a person you were.

Chapter 58

Be positive

I have always tried to live a happy, positive life. It was often a battle. We all have to cope with grief, depression and sorrows that may be inflicted by the death of a family member, a good friend or a serious ailment that can hit at any time. Times like these can be difficult for all of us to handle in the modern world. In most cases the medical experts will prescribe fistfuls of tablets or antidepressants to try to control it. In some cases, it works, at a price. Other non-medical experts may go with the old fashioned advice which may be more helpful and less expensive.

The ten bits of advice people often give are:

- Go for a 30 minute walk most days
- Eat and drink healthy
- Join a gym or a sports club
- To relax by reading
- Go dancing
- Take up gardening
- Take up a job you are happiest at
- Avoid rows and conflicts
- Stay in touch with family and friends
- Be happy and surround yourself with positive people

I have tried to do all these things. It's a battle at times, a war at other times and a total disaster at other times. Over the years I have tried to mix with positive people in order to stay positive. Negative people drag you down. Happy people make me happy and give me a laugh.

I was always into music and dancing. My favourite is country music. Last week I listened to Michael Commins' popular country music show on Midwest. It's the most popular country music show in Ireland and it can be picked up all over the world on various apps and websites. In the past the most popular country music show in Ireland was Pascal Mooney's country music show. The song 'Over the Years' reminds me of many of the exciting things in life that I reminisce about.

I was a bit of a 'poser' in my young days. We all like to show off our skills at dancing, singing or whatever. On one of these nights, I was asked to sing a song at a function where 600 people attended. I gave my version of 'The town I loved so well'. I got a standing ovation. After I left the stage a 'fan' approached me. She said, 'You have an amazing voice'. 'Do you think so?' I said. 'Yes,' she said. 'You have a grand soft voice like a cow.' That made my day. I was on tablets for the week.

The pain from grief

The pain from grief is hard to take
It hits you worse when you can't retreat
Like a hole in your heart that never fills
You wonder, you think where it all will end.

You lived a life so full of fun
You travelled the world and done your thing
But times will change for better or worse
You have no control when the going gets tough.

For years we talked about sickness and pain
We coped, we walked and looked at our gains
My mind was racing from place to place
Would the doctor's report be the same again?

You lived your life the best you can
You work, you cope surrounded by friends
With support around makes it all worthwhile
When life gets tough near the end of the line.

For life and death are much the same
You need friends to arrive and friends to go away
What matters most is what you made of your life
While fighting your way through this crazy mezzanine.

– Oliver Kelleher (2013)

Chapter 59

My life in business

I started my first business in 1976 with my late wife Mary. It was my lifelong ambition from when I sold my first two calves at ten years of age to set up my own business as soon as I had come to the use of reason. I spent a few years working in the business I loved. If you like what you do that, to me, was the most important part of any job I ever worked at. Since then, the business has prospered. It only lost money one year out of over 40 years in business. Starting any business can be a game of trial and error. Most people's success is built on luck. Oftentimes, the harder you work the luckier you get.

Two years after starting the business, I was advised to apply for an IDA grant for a manufacturing business we had started. We started a trophy and engraving business which came under the IDA umbrella that qualified for a grant. There was £10,000 of handy money that could give a boost to any small business, so I applied for it. I didn't realise I was about to get bogged down in red tape and bureaucracy. From day one I had to employ experts to do all sorts of feasibility studies, reports and projections. It got to the point where I spent more time writing reports for the IDA than I spent on the road writing orders. Maybe if we were getting €100,000 it would have made it worth the effort.

The grant process went into turbo. I had to supply the IDA with accounts and reports for a further ten years. One of the perks of the deal was if the business went out of business within ten years, we would have to pay back the grant in full. In hindsight it was a mistake to make this move instead of putting in the same time working with my staff to build the business without outside help. In fairness, I know many successful companies who wouldn't be around today if it were not for grants and incentives.

Ireland built its reputation on grants and tax incentives to many major businesses. In many cases it worked out very well because many of those major companies still operate here. Not everyone would agree Irish entrepreneurs get the attention or support they deserve. I have always believed that the best recipe for a successful economy is to attract foreign investment and promote local enterprise in tandem. In most cases small and large Irish businesses do business together by contacting the local manufacturers and supplying local products. This has worked extremely well because small and big businesses support one another by doing business with one another. This has worked well in the west and created a situation where many people can get work in their area and avoid the need to emigrate.

Chapter 60

Making good friends

From my earliest days in Castlebar I met up with people who are still good friends. These are people I would consult with if I had an issue in business where you would ask for advice. We would talk about the problems of the world. The things that are going arseways. Things that are being done well and things that could be done better.

We all have a topic to talk about or discuss. Some are topics that you can spend your life talking about, but it gets you nowhere regardless of how well your idea has been thought out or the simplicity of putting the plan in place.

Sometimes, I give up as it can wreck your head if you think too much about it. It's much worse if you know what you have in your mind will work and there is nobody there to listen to you. As I write the Irish government is in the process of trying to sell out rural Ireland to vulture funds to plant trees. I thought we put that out of our minds years ago after the British left this part of the world. Seemingly not. Certainly, it's a good idea to plant trees for the future to supply us with firewood when the Russians or others stop the supply of oil and gas to us. To me and many other normal people in Ireland, selling out to vulture funds is 'madness'.

Recently I met up with a Monaghan man, Paddy McGuinness, who has been a friend of mine since I left Leitrim and arrived in Castlebar. Over the years Paddy had played a big part in the Castlebar Song Contest and putting in place many more positive developments for the town in business and in politics. Every time we meet, we have a good conversation about what makes towns and businesses 'buzz'. It often boils down to the help, support and back up from everyone who can play a part in making any place great. We don't discuss high powered stuff that will cost millions to put in place. We don't talk about half doing a job and leaving the rest to someone else to take over. We talk about the simple, idiot-proof stuff that nearly always works if someone is prepared to run with it.

Paddy made one excellent observation about rural Ireland, climate change and the best way to approach the energy crisis or the cost of energy which is having an effect on every man, woman and child in Ireland. He put a suggestion to his political colleagues some time ago when he was a member of the council. His plan was to promote a grant aid for the growing of trees for firewood, not plant half of Ireland.

His idea to me and to most normal people would make a huge saving for hard pressed customers. Most farms in the west of Ireland have at least one acre that is good for nothing. It's either waterlogged, covered with nettles, weeds or not fit to farm. His suggestion was for every farmer who was interested, to plant this small piece of ground with trees for firewood. After a few years they will have an acre of firewood that will give them a cosy fire and heat water in an environmentally friendly fashion for their lifetime.

I'm not sure if Paddy's plan got a hearing at the time or would get a hearing if he proposed it today.

A positive move like that and a plan to look into the 100,000 empty houses across Ireland that could easily be made into liveable homes could be the start to solve our housing and our energy problems in a short time, for the long-term. It's not something that needs a lot of investment for the overall reward. It's something that needs get up and go by people with get up and go in them.

Maybe necessity would change people's minds and thinking in an era where we don't have too many simple solutions to serious problems. Only time will tell. Maybe we will have to wait until someone sees the light or until the lights go out.

For the record, statistics show that we have approximately €2 billion worth of timber suitable for firewood. These trees are in forests or along our roadsides or in fields and hedges across Ireland. These are trees and bushes that have fallen or are about to fall into fields or onto roads if a storm comes. All of these could be chopped up for firewood.

I'm told the government plan is to leave these trees on the ground to rot away to create a better environment for all of us down the road. Nothing about keeping our environment clean and safe for the present generation. Maybe the vulture funds operators will advise them on these issues, in secret, down the road.

Chapter 61

The mobile phone and smartphone era

As regards communicating, I didn't follow the flock and buy an array of the new gadgets for communication that hits the market every couple of years. I still use my upgraded version of the Nokia which I paid €35 for. It lets me know everything I want to know. I can call people on it; they can call me. They can text me and I can text them. They can leave a recorded message just as I can. Anything else in life I want to learn about I can pick up from talking to people, reading the papers and asking questions.

I sometimes get laughed at with my little Nokia. I often tell people I paid 3,500 for my phone. In most cases people say to me, 'Why did you give 3,500 for a phone?' The answer I give is, 'I couldn't get one any cheaper'. The next question I get is, 'Sure you can buy a phone for €40 or €50'. 'I know that', says I, 'But this one cost me 3,500 cents or €35'. It's only then that these people realise they know the price of many things we use every day. In most cases I don't leave them any the wiser. Common sense should make them more aware of the prices and value of things we need and things we did without for decades, and we still survived and prospered.

We have moved into a new world and are still moving where we know almost everything and remember very little. Some people know their own phone number and nobody else's. Other people cannot always remember their own number. That can happen in any walk of life. One story I was told about a wife who was checking out how good her husband's memory was. She asked him, 'Have you a good memory for faces?' 'I have,' he said. 'That's great,' said his wife, 'because I have just broken your shaving mirror'.

I always had a good memory for faces, but I still can't remember or recognise my own face when I'm shaving without a mirror. Am I unique? I'm not sure. I need to check it out with a mirror.

Who fears to speak

New sprawling homes cover the land
A sign that we are achievers
We turned our life and times around
Money, wealth and a sort of happiness
Looking after an open plan home
Not always an easy task

Everyone wants their own space
Yet nobody has space
Children toys and clothes everywhere
You can't hear your ears
Everyone talks together
You have to listen to so much at once

Children should be seen not heard
So, they used to say
Practice that now, you are a bad parent
Tell them to shut up you no longer can
You go with the flow and give in
That's parenting in an open plan home
Nothing wrong with that anymore

The topic is what's on the telly
Where's my iPad, where is my smartphone
Five year old shout out loud
Panic station, they're gone missing
Worse than losing your life
One of your arms has gone

For some it's the end of the world
For parents it's the stress of it all
For all of us it's the change of a generation
In your modern open plan home in the world

– *Oliver Kelleher* (2014)

Chapter 62

Memories of my hometown

My hometown of Mohill in County Leitrim and many more rural towns in the west were known for being prosperous market towns, both for retail business and fairs. This brought shoppers and cattle jobbers from many parts of Ireland because the choices were there in good, quality cattle and produce. Mohill had a great selection of businesses.

At the bottom of the town, Ivan Heuston ran a shop and filling station known as Houston Station. Booths owned a shop selling boots and shoes. Mervyn Lloyd still owns Lloyd's Insurance. Bill Body had a hardware and clothing shop selling body warmers to farmers. Luke Earley ran a pub and a late and early shop. Lattimers had a radio and tv shop. I believe a family of Kerrs owned a fruit and veg shop, selling Kerr's Pinks I presume.

The Crown family had the chemist and beauty shop selling medicines, ladies perfumes, hair pieces and crown toppers for the baldy men. Bradshaw and Clarke were wholesale grocers and builders providers, employing many people who later went on to set up their own businesses or went on to work as travelling salespeople for similar companies. One of the owners, Cecil Clarke, moved to Navan where he set up the first supermarket there in the '50s.

Quinn's of Mohill were known throughout Ireland. The business was set up by Joe Quinn who was an uncle of Pat Quinn (Quinnsworth). Joe bought up all the railway lines and sleepers that were being ripped up across the west. He sold these to farmers for bridges over drains and he used the tracks to build hay sheds.

Joe went on to establish Galco Steel in Dublin, which was the first galvanising plant in Ireland. P. Fitzpatrick was a schoolmaster in Aughavas. He setup a pub in Mohill. In the 1960s he built on a new lounge. His nephew came to do the official opening. He was Patrick McGoohan, who was born in Aughavas but the family moved to England when he was young. He went into acting and played the main part in the series Dangerman and The Prisioner on British TV. He was the highest paid actor in the UK in the 1960s. He later moved to America where he acted in the film Braveheart. He was offered the part of James Bond but he turned it down for personal reasons. He later went into film production and passed away a few years ago. Fitzpatrick's Céilí House is run by Val and Carmel Fitzpatrick. We can all look back on our own place and remember with pride and joy the great people who made things happen at a time when we had little money but great memories.

Chapter 63

My pet hates in life

All of us have pet hates in life. I'm no different to most people. You may not come up against these pet hates every day. That depends on what they are. One of my pet hates is to see people wasting money on food. My mother used to always say, 'Wilful waste makes woeful want'. We see this every day across the world where people don't have enough to eat while others have too much and dump out what they don't eat.

They claim that over 8 percent of all food that is purchased is dumped before it is even taken out of its packaging because it is gone past its sell by date. Another 5 percent is dumped because it is in the freezer for twelve months, you forget about it, and you may not know what is in the packet until it thaws out. The only time I empty my freezer is when I go away, and the power goes off or someone turns off or pulls out the plug of the freezer. The lot then goes in the bin.

If you run a business and you don't keep tabs on waste, you won't survive. One of the biggest losses in the hospitality and restaurant trade is waste. The profit can end up in the bin. Very few agencies nowadays train people how to manage and control waste. While many agencies show people how to save on electricity, gas and energy, you are seldom shown how to buy food on a budget. Common sense should tell us how to do these things, but common sense isn't always common. I don't like to see people spending other people's money as if there were no tomorrow and the well will never run dry.

We see that around us a lot, but we often can do feck all about it only complain. When you have to perfect the art of survival in business to pay your staff and all the others who are demanding their share out of your business, you need to sharpen the pencil and sharpen your skills without becoming an unbearable bore.

Politicians and governments can justify a lot of the money they spend, whether part of it is wasted or well-spent. That's known as bureaucracy, which is another way of doing things differently. In recent years we have seen politicians cutting the tape on many new enterprise centres around the country. Most of them cost a lot of money and are a disaster, others cost little and are huge successes. The flagship of these are the various greenways, blueways and redways we opened across the country so people can get out and cycle, walk or run in the open air to stay healthy. It was a no brainer but someone with brains had to come up with the idea. Like our lakes, rivers and canals, they are a huge asset that should be protected.

For some people, pet hates include stupid drivers who don't know the rules of the road because they were brought up in an era where you applied for a driver's licence and got one even if you didn't know how to drive.

I have a licence to drive a high-powered truck with a 40-foot container behind it even though I am not able, or would I chance driving a truck without a 40-foot container behind it. If I had applied for a licence 40 years ago when I was a young fella to drive a jumbo jet, I could be winging my way around the world dropping travellers off in airports all around the globe. I didn't apply for the pilot's licence and I don't plan to at this stage of my life.

Many of us go through a lot of traumas with bad drivers, reckless drivers, inconsiderate drivers, stupid drivers and ignorant drivers. Recently, as I was going around a roundabout, a stupid driver zoomed out in front of me and I was forced to brake hard as he drove onto the roundabout, into my path. He let down his window and gave me a mouthful of abuse as to why I drove out in front of him. I blew him a kiss and told him that he should yield to traffic coming from the right on a roundabout. Not impressed with my romantic gesture he gave me another mouthful and drove off.

These types of things don't upset me too much. Neither does the antics of many wired up people.

Despite all this, there are things which drive me dafter than others. Perhaps my greatest pet hate is flat packed furniture, or, should I say, trying to assemble flat packed furniture. I'm gone past that now, having had some disastrous experience trying to assemble items. I was never trained to do this simply because I never wanted to be trained. I'd prefer to buy a wardrobe or a dressing table already assembled so I know exactly what I'm paying for.

In the fancy showrooms that specialise in flatpacks, they sit you down and offer you a coffee. The implications of the whole experience were unbelievable, watching the video of how our dream kitchen should work. The only thing that seemed to be missing was the Michelin Star chef that came with the kitchen.

It was a very impressive sales pitch and I asked what size van or truck did I need to transport the stuff to my home?

I was told it will fit into a small van because it was a flat pack kitchen that arrived from China to Ireland in eight flat pack boxes of timber panels, five boxes of dowels, door handles and skimpy timber beading, 12 boxes of screws and 35 pages of instructions you would need binoculars to read from any distance.

I was confused.

Could I buy the kitchen like you have it displayed in the showroom?

No, that's only for display and we get one of these assembled in the factory in China with every 40-foot container of timber panels, screws, dowels and wrenches so you can assemble it in the comfort of your own home.

So, the product on display was priced at €2,800 but the true facts were you were not allowed to buy the real product. You get 25 boxes of timber panels, screws, nuts, bolts and instructions and you fit it in during your spare time just to keep you amused over the Christmas.

A great new modern way to keep ourselves amused provided you don't lose or mislay the instructions or a box of screws.

At least if the job doesn't work out where you are trying to assemble the unit, you can always post up the photo on the box of maybe what it will look like when you get around to assembling the apparatus. If it doesn't work out, you can always use the timber over the winter as fuel for the fire, even though it's difficult to burn compressed timber shavings mixed with glue.

So, you could say, and I certainly can say, that one of my pet hates is assembling flat pack furniture that has more than two screws.

To check out if I was the only one in the world who wasn't a fan of flat pack furniture, I called to a neighbour who had bought a flat pack bed. He took on the job of assembling it on his own. After four hours of frustration, cursing and swearing, he decided he just couldn't handle it. Before I went down to the room to oversee the operation, his wife advised me not to go down to the room if I didn't want the head taken off me.

He was in the room for two and a half hours and still no sign of a bed appearing. He was well set up, screws, nuts, bolts, bed head, spring base, top base, bottom base and two side poles to keep the parts together.

I advised him he should get another expert to work with him as it was a two-person job. I should have kept my trap shut because in frustration he nearly blew a gasket and told me where to go. I retreated to the luxury of the sitting room and swallowed a cup of coffee without making any more efforts or moves to solve the crisis. It was an experience buying the family bed, but it was a greater experience trying to assemble it. We all think we are capable of doing anything in life that looks simple watching an expert doing.

These are some of the pitfalls of modern day shopping. We all know the price of everything because of the internet and online shopping. It can be difficult to know the value of anything if the product is half made when you buy it with a set of assembly instructions that you may not even understand and be able to follow. Anyway, if it keeps us amused and out of trouble, maybe it's worth it.

Chapter 64

The writing bug

I spent over six years writing an opinion column for *The Connaught Telegraph* and the *Western People*. Once the bug hit me, I couldn't stop. I was always on the lookout for a good story that people in any part of Ireland or the world would be interested in reading.

At the same time, I started writing poems. Short poems that usually took me no more than 15 minutes to write. Once I started to write a poem or my columns for the papers, I had to keep writing. If I left down the pen, it would take me two days to get the inspiration and the words to finish. It usually took me about one hour to write 1,600 words with my pen and paper. It would take me another hour to read and correct the spellings before it went to print.

Nowadays we see celebrities, actors, chefs, musicians, comedians and people of every walk in life who want to write a book. People like to talk, tell stories and jokes. That's why many are inspired to write a book.

While writing for the newspapers, some people told me I used to be controversial and the same people told me I always told the truth and said what needed to be said. My approach was to tell it as it is. Don't point the finger at someone who works in a job where things are done arseways. The people who work in these jobs are not the people who write the rules on how they and the systems work. For that reason, we shouldn't blame individuals who are only following rules and regulations that were antiquated and out of date. Sadly, we are inclined to shoot the messenger instead of trying to change the systems that don't work. Obviously, we should complement people operating systems that do work well, and we have many of them.

Chapter 65

The Creamers of Leitrim

One of my best friends in national school was Ray Creamer whose family lived and worked on Lough Rynn estate for a lifetime. Ray was the quiet one in the class. It was a good job there was someone who gave Master McKenna and Mrs McLaughlin peace. When we finished school, I went onto secondary school to try to better myself. My father used to call that, 'Trying to make something out of me'.

Ray later moved to Mohill. He emigrated like his brothers did and ended up in London where he sadly passed away in 2022. The Creamers were probably among the most famous people to come out of Leitrim. The three brothers, Ray, Des and Liam were in the Guinness Book of Records. They competed in Tug of War for Luton and England and went on to win not one but nine world titles.

Most of the old country schools are now closed, overgrown by bushes and trees. My old school was kept open as a centre after they built the new school beside it. It is still standing and in a good structural state. It's sad to see so many well-built schools being left to rot when they could have been given to the local recreational centres. This is something that should not have happened just as we should not have let our old railway station houses go to rack and ruin. Politicians took a peculiar approach to many things the British built.

We took the same approach to looking after our lakes, rivers and canals. We never maintained them even though we have politicians ranting on about how to save the planet and hopefully save ourselves.

Was it a case of getting everything British out of Ireland? Why did we not have the cop on to hold onto what suited and get rid of what didn't suit? In my own home parish in Leitrim, Lough Rynn Castle was restored and now houses a top class, four star hotel.

All of the houses, outhouses and fine, stone-built limekiln dispensaries, churches and schools which Lord Leitrim built are still standing and occupied by locals or foreigners from Dublin who settled in the area to take part in fishing activities or boating on the Shannon.

We developed the Shannon for up to 2,000 boats and cruisers who travel through the lakes, canals and rivers on cruise holidays. These actually have created huge business for all the towns on these lakes and rivers with over 100 restaurants opening in less than 20 years.

My next project is to spend three months doing a world tour of Leitrim, Fermanagh, Roscommon, Westmeath, Offaly, Clare and Limerick by boat. Chances are it will rain most days so I will bring my raingear to save me from the elements we get here in the west. Great, healthy outdoors always appeal to me and when it rains all you have to do is put on your raincoat. Look out for me if you happen to see me 'thumbing' on the road. Chances are the boat ran out of diesel, it broke down or it sank. All of these happened to me in the past. It still didn't put me off my adventures in life.

For now, and for many years, I have settled in Castlebar in Co Mayo. For many years my business has taken me to most of the counties in Ireland and abroad. They still tell me I haven't lost my flat Leitrim accent. I am a bit of an expert on accents now because everyone I meet up with, I ask them, 'Where are you from?' I'm told you are not allowed to ask people that question anymore in case you offend them.

I have been asking it for so long now so I will find it difficult to stop now. I will probably end up being looked upon as being a 'racist' for asking these types of questions. Certainly not by my friends who are made up of black, white, Indian, coloured and Hispanic in all walks of life.

Chapter 66

The house of the rising sun

There is one way to destroy a good friendship – invite them out to stay in your new holiday home in Spain or Turkey. For months in advance, you tell them about your new holiday home in Spain, where it's situated on the side of a mountain overlooking the Atlantic Ocean, six-minute walk from the beach and restaurants and about ten minutes from the Olde Town. You listen with your mouth open wondering where they got the money to buy it. They must have done well in the bad times; someone left them a lob of money or was it money from that offshore account the taxman never heard about? Before you visit, it's often like listening to a long-playing record that never seems to end. You hear about the Irish pub owned by some criminal who made his money from drug dealing and is now permanently resident in Spain who might tell you he would never come back to live in this 'kip of a country' again.

Then you hear about the neighbours, the couple down the road from Galway who are very nice. You meet up with them in the Irish pub and you talk about all the things that are happening back home, what the government is doing to get the country back on track and what they are not doing that's making a bollocks of the place. You're never stuck for a word or a chat. Then you have the other couple who go out of their way to converse and talk to you. Chances are if you lived next door to them in Ireland, they wouldn't bid you the time of day because they may feel they are more part of a different type of society back home.

After months of coaxing and several invitations, one decides I have to go out and see how the other half live, those who can afford holiday homes in the sun.

You may be pleasantly or unpleasantly surprised when you arrive.

Two hours' drive from the airport and you arrive in Savadora. A one horse town on the side of a mountain. A few half dilapidated shops, bars and ladies' hairdressers. These were built in the boom to cater for all the well-heeled Irish rich who were supposed to move into the 'Sale Agreed' holiday homes which are half full and half empty, half built or not built at all.

You had your choice, and you paid the same price to the builder regardless of which one you bought. It was cash up front in most cases and if you were one of the lucky original investors, you got your hands on one that may have been badly finished, complete with a garden full of rock that you could break your neck over trying to get in the front or back door.

What about it? Ireland was booming and any of the banks that operated in the cash rich principality of Ireland was only too eager to give you 100 percent loans to buy up 'to keep up with the Joneses'. At the same time Ireland was in the grip of 'cruiser mania'. To complement the holiday home in Spain and stay part of the Joneses, you bought your cruiser and launched on the Shannon.

You were now part of the real Ireland that our politicians boasted about. It was this image that others talked about throughout Europe. In the European Parliament we were held up as role models – 'why can't you ludremauns be like the Irish?' The most prosperous little country in the world. We were building houses as if they were never going to go out of fashion. But they were going to go out of fashion. We built 230,000 more than we needed and now nobody wants to live in them even though they may get them for nothing. They want other houses like the cruiser and the holiday home in Spain.

We sort of lost interest in the material things in life, especially when you can't pay the repayments on them. The bankers came looking for you. Not you but your money. So, you have no money. So, the holiday home in Spain and the cruiser on the Shannon bites the dust. They say there are always two great days with a cruiser and a holiday home. One is the day you buy it and the other is the day you sell it.

I decided in 2009 to take a friend up on his invitation to his stately holiday home on the coast in Spain. It wasn't what I expected. It was what I thought. My friend bought the house off the plans from a reputable Irish agent, so he hadn't a bull's notion what it was like or where exactly it was. The photos taken from the seas below were like something from the movies. The photo from the home to the sea looked like a mountain that had had gorse fires every week of the year.

We arrived and my fears were realised. It was situated a mile up a mountain that without a car or any public service transport, the only way to the home would be to jump on one of stray asses and hope you'll make it there safely. We arrive at the holiday home; drop off our rucksacks and spare clothes and head downhill, walking to the pub. No problem walking down the hill.

We arrived into the Irish pub in the town where everyone behind the bar spoke German or Polish. In the space of two hours, we slugged down four or five pint of well mixed Guinness that had travelled like us from Dublin. At 11.30pm we head for the hills, no streetlights, no taxis, no way of knowing which way to turn in the dark. We even forgot to leave the light on in the house on the hill for direction.

My journey into the mountain with seven pints on board was a memorable one. I thought I was having a nightmare looking at stray asses and goats staring at me and sore feet from the rocky, uneven road. The good thing about it was I couldn't remember how bad the experience was trying to climb the rocks with an over-supply on board. All the rest I will leave to your imagination because I'm glad I have forgotten it by now.

My bit of advice now is if you feel like buying a holiday home in the sun, buy it now while the going is good as we still could be living in the best little country in the world depending on which way you look at it. From the seas or from the mountains, the choice is yours to enjoy it.

Chapter 67

A trip to the Costa Brava

I have happier memories of a trip to the Costa Brava in Spain to lap up the food, the sun and to do a bit of business there. It's only over two hours from Ireland West Airport, Knock to Girona. From the minute you land you feel you're in a different world. And you are. The sun shines there for longer than it does in Ireland. Drink and fags are much cheaper than anywhere in Ireland which is all part of the EU. Twenty cigarettes are about €6, a six pack of that woeful-tasting lager costs €1.40, that's about 25c a bottle. You could afford to get drunk every day for less than a fiver. Despite that, I didn't come across one drunk, anti-social, bad mouthed, unruly individual in my seven day stay even though I was socialising at 2 o'clock in the morning. Maybe if I went to other parts of Palomas where I was staying, I might have contacted them.

Police patrol the streets day and night either on motor bikes, cars or police vans. They seem to stop regularly to talk to people or give directions to lost tourists. They seem to be very well kitted out with computers in the back of their cars, vans or bikes. Maybe that's the way it works everywhere in the EU. All police carry batons and guns, for security I presume. I didn't see or speak to anyone who felt intimidated by the fact that they could be shot or battered with a baton. The only people who might be intimidated would be those who would want to attack the police. Obviously, these people may be put off from attacking someone who is carrying a gun or a baton. Obviously, it's more effective pointing a gun at a thug who is going to attack them than pointing a biro at them.

So, should police be armed with guns and batons? In a country like Ireland, where it doesn't happen, it may seem like a draconian move. In countries where it already exists, it's the normal way of policing and in many cases, it works better than threatening a thug by pointing a biro at him and giving him a warning. Our crime rates in Ireland have exploded mainly because the sale and use of illegal drugs, gangland operators and drug related crime has gone out of control. I think the butt of a pencil or the biro is gone well past its use by date and it's not working. I'm not saying guns and batons will solve everything. They will solve nothing unless the people in charge take their responsibilities seriously. Nobody knows when serious crime will level off. It never does, especially if it's easy to get into the trade.

While I felt very safe as did the thousands of young and old tourists who walk the streets of many busy resorts across Europe, you get the impression that gangland stuff and drug dealing are kept well out of the limelight to protect their only real economy which is tourism. Spain is a vast country where parts of it are rife with drug dealing and crime. Despite that, Catalonia, which is part of North East Spain, seems to have much more control on how to look after their own and look after tourists that travel in their millions there every year.

I was very impressed by the way the people of Catalonia do business. I asked in a shop for a map of Spain. 'Not available, only maps of Catalonia'. It was my first time in this resort and it certainly impressed me how a simple formula can work to make a place beautiful and safe to walk the streets or the beaches at any time of the day or night and without falling over rubbish, butts of fags or beer cans. These things can work well anywhere if people put a plan in place and follow that plan.

Then again Catalonia, which Barcelona is the main city, is the most prosperous part of Spain and pays huge amounts into the national coffers. Is it any wonder they want their own independence? They seem to have a common sense plan to do a lot of things that help businesses and create business. In the busy resort of Platja d'Aro there is more business done on the streets in marketplaces or in purpose-built retail outdoor centres than they do in shopping centres. On Friday morning I visited an outdoor market with 280 stalls selling everything from clothes, footwear, dry foods, meat and fish. On one fish stall there were twelve people employed selling over 65 different types of fish out in the open. To get your place in the queue you had to pull your ticket. Market yards, public areas and areas are owned by the people. This could create a whole new business venture for bricks and mortar retailers who find it hard to get customers in their doors. If this is the case which it is in many towns and villages in rural Ireland, then it's time to think outside the shop and let people set up on our footpaths and pedestrianise streets for the days and areas these businesses operate in. We have a long way to go to get any politician or civil servant to think like this regarding the damage they are doing to town centres everywhere.

Street trading was part of our tradition for generations. I bought my first calf on the street in Mohill when I was twelve. No point in going into a shop to buy him. I bought my first chicken, duck and eggs on the street not out of a freezer wrapped in a plastic bag with another lump of plastic inside it with the giblets and a plastic tie wrap to seal it and then have it fired into another plastic bag. Is it time that business took back their towns and did business that is best suited to them and their customers? It could be a restart for many people who produce eggs, milk, garlic, cabbage, onions and many of the things we import and for them to be given a chance to sell their own freshly grown Irish products on the streets. The best way to put my plan into practice is to fill ten Ryanair planes, fly 100 politicians and 100 public servants from Knock to Catalonia, Poland and Italy and show them how things work in 20 European countries and can work in Ireland too. Will it ever happen? I don't know. Maybe with Britain having finally left the EU, we might start thinking outside the box and put plans in place for Irish businesses to prosper without the need for red tape and stumbling blocks that destroy great businesses and great economies. I think we've seen it all and it could be a good time to think twice about the way we could do business better.

It could be our last opportunity to give Ireland back to the people who matter, using a bit of cop on and common sense which as a rule doesn't cost money to provide or implement.

A lot of these types of ideas could snowball to bring back life into Irish towns. Ballina runs a very successful Salmon Festival where thousands of locals and returned immigrants take their holidays to coincide with the event. The streets are closed, and traffic diverted (which is a very simple plan to put in place) and the town is buzzing with excitement. It's a time that people meet up and talk about things that matter. Last time I visited this festival I had my usual annual meet up with Eddie Melvin, Ollie Rouse and the late Betty Sweeney where we talked about almost everything. Brexit, Donald Trump, Theresa May and Irish government problems are usually not on our menu. The only thing we didn't do was to convince the Russians to stay out or get out of Afghanistan. Obviously, that's for another day and I'm working on it. We'll leave these major problems to the experts who have an answer to everything.

The street trading I saw taking place in the Spanish tourist resorts was an inspiration to me in how simple it is to create business when people are given half a chance. It gives them the opportunity to sell products they produce in a friendly, happy environment in the open. Even if it rains, which we all think is the greatest drawback to doing any business in Ireland, you can buy an umbrella or a raincoat for as little as a fiver. Not only do people selling goods make money but customers and children can have a great day out that is totally different to sitting at home on a smartphone watching cartoons or what's going wrong with the world.

It could be a great opportunity to promote recycling like I saw in Costa Brava towns. The local council had skips at every point to collect plastic, paper and other waste. The whole area was extremely tidy with designated areas for boxes and plastic to be sorted for collection three or four times during the day. I noticed 90 percent of the waste was made up of cardboard and waste and cut offs of vegetables which were discarded into another bin to recycle into compost. Compost and peat moss are the most popular products after flowers and vegetables to be used in any garden. Ireland has millions of tons of both. Is there an opportunity to sell these two products in our street markets where you bring your own recyclable bag and fill it from a bulk compost container just like you can go into your co-op and buy a trailer load of meal in bulk or buy a trailer load or a bag of sand from the local quarry?

Chapter 68

People watching and surveys

Every time I go on my travels, I do a few daft things. To me they may not be daft but to the ordinary traveller or holiday maker they may seem somewhat daft. Most people who travel to Spain go there for the sun just to get away from the fecking rain in Ireland. The weather doesn't bother me here in Ireland because when it rains here all you have to do is put on a coat and away you go with a cheap brolly. I must say I don't like to see rain in Spain simply because you don't expect it to rain in Spain.

At one time I liked air travel even though I hate airports. They are the most depressing, challenging places you could ever be forced to go to. Passengers waiting with long faces, the case in one hand, the mobile phone in the other and their boarding pass in their mouth if they don't have it on their smartphone. Do I have my passport, you check twenty times and every time you find it in a different pocket. To me that's the worst experience to have or to watch as you struggle through customs into the duty free where they will spray all sorts of quare stuff on you just to get you to buy some cheap eau de cologne.

Through customs, you head off down escalators that are turned off, but you still walk on them in the hope they might start, and you get a chance to rest your legs. One long corridor into another, you're nearly back in Dublin city by the time you get to the steps that whisk you off to the plane. You're on your way to Barcelona, the capital of Catalonia.

I'm not a man of the big city scene. Big cities are the same everywhere. Traffic and more traffic and everyone addressing you in a foreign language and make sure you don't cross on a pedestrian crossing especially if you are drunk. Anyway, if you're drunk you shouldn't be on the road.

Some of the daft things I usually get up to when I'm travelling around the world is to sit and watch people's antics and behaviour. So, this time I started at Dublin Airport watching the goings on and behaviour of people. This time my survey was on how many people queuing up to board a flight were smiling or laughing. Out of 1,000 I surveyed I wasn't shocked but surprised because, wait for it, only 55 people out of 1,000 were smiling and only three out of those were laughing that you could hear. Amazingly out of 400 children who were with parents or guardians in the queues, 200 were smiling. An interesting result from a survey that should see a lot of people smiling or laughing because they were 90 percent probably going on holidays. Sadly, we now see travel, especially air travel, as a real downer because of regulations on what you can or can't bring with you. Well that's the price you pay for cheap dinners. You still can book a luxury flight anywhere, but you still have the same restrictions.

I arrived in Barcelona Airport and a weight is lifted off my shoulders because I'm on holidays, away from Christmas shoppers who already have started panic buying back home, just in case the shops run out of turkey, ducks, geese, ham, chickens, sausage meat and bread. We would all starve at Christmas without them.

I'm on the train heading north to Ripoll about two hours north of Barcelona. It's a republican town of approximately 30,000 people. Six of their citizens are locked up in prison because they are demanding independence for Catalonia while former Catalonian leader, Carles Puigdemont, is now in exile in Belgium. The people of Catalonia are friendly people. On the streets of Ripoll, you will find women and children huddled on street corners having the banter like we did in Ireland a few years ago or before modern technology took over. Most people you meet on the streets will greet you with a wave and 'hola' (hello). The town centre in Ripoll is busy because there are over 10,000 people still living within the town. Most of the shopping centres are within the town or in the markets area which gives a great buzz to any county town in any country. I wandered through markets, shops, pubs and restaurants on busy streets and quaint side streets that were built 2,000 years ago and are still standing and home to many people.

I decided after day two to conduct another survey. This time it was on 2,000 people in Ripoll and the way they behave and what their social life is made up of. So, I'm observing people on mobile phones, smartphones or some of the many gadgets that people are glued to as they rush along streets or simply fiddle with when they are eating a meal or drinking a coffee. The survey was, 'How many people out of 1,000 had a mobile device in their hand or were talking or texting on the yoke?' It was a shock result as I found out when I arrived back in Ireland and asked my friends what they thought the figure might be. Some said 900 out of 1,000 would be on smartphones or some other phone; others said 800, 600, 500. The closest answer was 250 out of 1,000. The actual figure was 35 out of 1,000. Most people were shocked at the result but very few disputed it. They simply thought that every person across the world is hooked on mobile phones and smartphones which is not the case. Maybe that's why when you travel to many parts of the world you see people doing business selling goods and looking after customers without having to resort to any mobile device. This used to be called GCS, good customer service, which still appeals to me and most people no matter where you do business.

After I came home, I read where shares in Apple dropped to their lowest in a year because the sale of phone smartphones has dropped. Obviously, people may be realising that it's cheaper to talk than it is to send a message on a thousand euro gadget that doesn't always do the job you expect from it.

Chapter 69

Going as far away as possible

One New Year, I decided to head off to some hot spot in some other part of the world for a bit of sunshine and see how the other half live. I picked the furthest point that I could travel to on this planet earth, from Castlebar.

After leaving Castlebar I headed for London, on to Singapore, on to Melbourne and eventually ending up in Auckland in New Zealand over 30 hours later. I did the usual things you're told to do on a long trip. Take a sleeping tablet and wear a pair of those white nylon socks so it saves you from blood clots. The sleeping tablets didn't work because I spent 28 out of the 30 hours awake wondering would the sleeping tablets work. They didn't. I resorted to other ways of making me sleep. Counting sheep. New Zealand, like Ireland, is a big producer of sheep. They rear over 23 million sheep every year as against Ireland's 2.5 million.

Counting 20 sheep in a field can be a relatively easy job but counting imaginary sheep 35,000 feet up in the air can be a battle and a long drawn out process. Counting 23 million sheep takes a bit longer. I did my sums to try and establish how long it would take to count 23 million sheep. At 60 per minute that would work out at 86,400 per day or 604,800 per week. So, it would take me nearly 38 weeks to count all the sheep in New Zealand and there was still no guarantee I would fall asleep.

I arrived in Auckland having flown over the bush fires that were raging in the forests below us. The fires were engulfing an area the size of Ireland. Many lives were lost and over $5 billion worth of damage was done and the fires are still burning. It took a huge toll on the wildlife which is more or less sacred in these parts of the world. My favourite little animal, the koala bear, was wiped out in some parts. The bear lives in the trees and most of their habitat was ablaze with nowhere safe for them to run to.

The heat in Auckland was about 40 degrees when I arrived. Days before trains were not running because of the danger of tracks overheating. For my first two nights in Auckland I had the pleasure of sleeping in a hotel bed with all the comforts. I spent two days in Auckland city studying how the rest of the world performs and how a country like New Zealand can survive out in the middle of nowhere, over 2,000 km away from their nearest neighbour. Auckland looks a bit like most cities in the world of its size. They run a tight ship and your chances of ending up at the airports and hoping to get in to avail of their social welfare system or any other system, is nil. You may be able to get there as a stowaway on a plane or in a 40ft container, if you could survive the heat. Even if you do make it you may be sent home the next day.

Despite the fact that Auckland is a prosperous city, I was amazed at the amount of people begging on the streets or huddled in corners with blankets over them. I'm told they don't have a homeless crisis despite the fact that they have people begging on the streets and sleeping out. I went on tour one night to meet up with some of these people. I found a few hard luck individuals who hadn't had a home for years. I came across more people who found it worthwhile to sit on a corner begging. One gentleman I spoke to, who was begging, told me his circumstances when I asked him about his lifestyle. 'Do you have a home to go to tonight?' I asked. 'Yes, I have an apartment four miles down the road, and I'm moving into a new one here in the city in two weeks'. I asked him if he was getting any state welfare which he said amounted to $220 New Zealand dollars per week. Why, I asked, are you begging? 'I need a lot of money to buy furniture for the new apartment when I move in.'

To me he looked like someone who could work to earn money. He didn't have to work, he told me, because he could pick up more begging in a few hours tax free, than working. I asked him if the begging business and homeless business were a bit of a racket. He agreed with me that some people do abuse it. After half an hour he picked up the plastic container, emptied the money into his pocket and headed home.

New Zealand is certainly not a welfare state, but they have held onto some of the old British systems that prevail in some parts of the world today.

I'm back in my room in the hotel. It's bedtime. I can't sleep with the heat and thinking about the fact that I'm probably in the wrong job to make handy money. Counting sheep won't solve any of these problems for me. The tablets aren't working either so I could end up walking around the room for the night thinking of the snow, frost, rain and high winds back at home. It worked.

Like New York, they do things big out here. Off-licences here in New Zealand are not next door to a pub. They are in supermarkets covering 20,000 or 30,000 square feet that sell nothing but drink, alcoholic drink included. All the old and modern tower blocks of apartments or offices have multi-storey car parks downstairs. Nearly all the city centre and suburbs of Auckland offer free parking for up to two hours. In certain prime high streets, you could pay up to $10 per hour to park. The beauty is you have the choice.

I'm on my way by boat from Auckland to Coromandel, a wild west style town with a gold mining history. This was the second largest town in the North Island of New Zealand at one time. It was a busy place at the time of the gold rush but today the population has tumbled to less than 2,000 people. They have kept all the old character. The old pub fronts and the hotel signs on buildings that are not hotels. They are pubs that were once hotels in the gold rush era and planning laws here state they have to leave the old signage in situ as part of their heritage. You won't see any international supermarkets or department stores in Coromandel. Up in the mountains are the remains of old mine shafts where people once used to dig out iron ore and search for gold that might have made them rich. Today, it seems to be more difficult to find gold than it has been in the past.

As a rule, people dig gold out of a hole in the ground and turn it into a very valuable product. They then sell it at about $1,600 per ounce to a willing purchaser. They then give it to someone else who digs another hole in the ground and buries the gold in it for safe-keeping.

I'm heading south to a campsite in the middle of nowhere. On a bus across mountains, down dirt track roads surrounded by vines and grapes. The vegetation is burned brown in parts because of the lack of regular rain. There is more dry yellow soil than grass. There are more 40 shades of green here than in Ireland, without the whins, the nettles, the ragwort or the heather. They can still run prosperous farms here and get a reasonable price for their produce. Despite that many farmers told me they are planning on moving out of sheep because there is more money in growing grapes, vines, avocados and more exotic fruits which there is more demand for worldwide. Could Irish farmers learn a lesson from the Kiwis and move away from producing goods where they have no control or say in the price they get for their produce.

Amazingly over here in restaurants you will see a sirloin steak on the menu priced at the market value on the day. Unlike Ireland the price to the farmer for meat can change on a regular basis depending on demand. I better go as my 16oz sirloin steak is burning on the barbecue.

Chapter 70

Doing our bit to save the Earth

In the past decade a lot of lobby groups and save the planet people have come up with a vast amount of ways of doing that. From plans to stop cows farting to horses dunging in fields and on roads. There are thousands of proposals to save the earth and save ourselves. The latest one which we should have looked at 50 years ago is how to handle waste, recycle waste and dump waste. We are not good at that because there are more plastic bottles and beer cans in the oceans than there are people in the world, and we cannot seem to be able to get to the bottom of it or on top of it. We do a lot of talking about these things. We are, in fairness, good at talking and having talks about talks. At least we are engaging, which is good, even if you achieve nothing.

The US state of Washington has gone a few steps further in the quest to save the ozone layer. It's the first state to legalise human composting after its eco-friendly governor signed a new law in a bid to end carbon emissions from burials and cremations. So, I am sure you would like to know how you can donate your body (after you die) for composting purposes. Firstly, you will need a garden, a plot of land, a flower bed or a few flowerpots. You will need a spade and bucket and maybe a wheelbarrow. When you die in the state of Washington you will have the option to donate your body to mother earth by having it transferred into soil that will be suitable for use in your garden or someone else's garden. The process is called recomposition. Obviously, you will have to make these plans before you die. There was only one fella we know of who came back after he died to give us all lectures on mortality. Obviously, if he opted for recomposition there would be no word about him today.

Recomposition will replace embalming, burials and cremations and you will save a rake of money and turn yourself into some use-

ful purpose, something many don't do when they are alive. I'd
nearly run with the idea just to see and taste the flavour of toma-
toes and onions grown with the Kelleher Brand of Compost. One
expert put it nicely when he said, 'The idea of returning to nature
so directly and being beautifully brought back into the cycle of life
and death is actually pretty beautiful'. Incidentally, the speaker of
those words was Katrina Spade (if you pardon the pun), she was
the woman who lobbied for the law to be changed.

So how will they compost me if I agree to go down that garden?
Will they dump me in a compost heap like mushroom manure and
keep me in the dark for months covered in you know what? I'm
not sure if I can choose the type of compost I would like to be reincarnated into. Obviously, my first choice would be a rose compost as I like rose trees. Then again, I could by being turned into a
cabbage or banana fertiliser where I could give something back to
the hungry people of the world and the monkeys could gorge
themselves on my own brand of bananas.

The inventor of the idea, Katrina Spade, is to shovel you into a
steel container, obviously with no holes in it. Slam the lid on it and
in 30 days you're ready for the cabbage plot. The end product will
look like you would see in any nursery around Mayo, your teeth
and bones would all be used as fertiliser. There is nothing new in
this process. They have been using it for years with farm animals
and it is socially acceptable in many parts. The cost in America to
get the human version of this is about $5,500 (€5,200 or £4,500). I
presume you can bring the bag of compost home with you for that
price. I'm not sure what the Catholic Church thinks about this or
the undertaker, solicitor or all the others who make money out of
us when we die. I'm not sure right now whether I will opt for this
form of extermination. I'm not going to advise you on which route
to go either. For the minute my main concern in life is to stay alive
and happy and try not to destroy the world for all these people who
think the same.

Chapter 71

Food, glorious food and what it's like to be vegan

Growing up as a young fella, my mother never had much problem getting me to eat my meals. If I didn't eat them fast some other member of the family would have it eaten for me. I was always a food and drink lover, because I always believe you won't survive without either. For years I cooked food and ate the food I cooked. I was always careful not to destroy a good steak after I paid good money for it. Having to throw good food in the bin annoys me and when I see it happen, I often feel like saying, why not keep that and use it tomorrow. When I say that I'm usually told where to go and get a life. So, for many reasons I keep my trap shut and say nothing.

In recent times veganism seems to be getting a lot of coverage in the media. When some notable celebrity or politician says meat is not good for you, it causes a stir and we all want to hear their story. Their story becomes a platform for animal lovers who don't want any animals or birds killed so you vultures can cook them and eat them. Amazingly, none of the people ever object to people using a trap or poison to catch or kill rats or mice. Do they not deserve to live a life like the turkey, chicken or pig? Another day you read where you shouldn't buy coffee or tea from certain countries that use cheap labour. Nor should we buy fruit and vegetables from countries that are being run by dictators. Only recently we heard where the Irish government were looking at banning food and other commodities from Israel, because they refused to recognise Jerusalem as the capital of Israel. Where will all this end? I don't know but trying to get Irish people to stop eating Irish meat is taking it a bit far.

Recently I read an article from So Vegan about how meat can cause serious harm. I suppose lack of meat and lack of food can cause more harm to the world. Cigarettes are bad for us, too much alcohol is bad for us, contaminated water is bad for us, eating fish that lives on a diet of plastic bags and chemical waste in the seas is bad for us, emissions from all the toxic waste in the world is bad for us and bad for this place we call home, the Earth.

So, where do we start to save ourselves? Will giving up meat save the world? Animals and birds will still be around so will they start to eat us instead? Obviously, we could easily become a treat because in a few years we would have ten times more animals and birds in the world than humans so, I would be afraid to be around if I saw ten wild boars and 100 wild turkeys looking in the window at me in the morning looking for food. Obviously, if we cannot feed and house humans, what chance have we of feeding hungry cows, sows, bears and wild turkeys? Don't please tell me I have the answer to these questions too.

Food to most people is a passion, either preparing it, cooking it or eating it. There are millions of cookery books sold every year around the world. There are hundreds of TV shows on the art of cooking and eating and there seems to be no let-up in the appetite people have for watching, reading and studying these. Recently, one country politician suggested that any man that doesn't eat lumps of meat every day would be a useless man in the bog, driving a digger around the fields of Kerry or shovelling cow dung out of cattle sheds. I sort of believe him. When Healy-Rae made the comments, he was talking from experience or maybe he was looking at the job performance of the people who were suggesting they were cutting down on meat. In fairness if the same people ate two or three boiled eggs before they started their day this might give them the energy and egg them on to perform with a meat intake.

For years there were foods I would never attempt to eat simply because I didn't like the look of them, or I felt I wouldn't like them. As time went by, I started to look at these foods and try them out. So, the likes of home cooked lasagne or hot curry chicken or doner kebabs are now some of my favourites. Sorry veganites, they all contain meat. I still like my Caesar salads, my boxty, burgers and good old Irish roast lamb or roast beef. So far, they haven't convinced me that the world can live on vegetables they grow in Spain, Italy, France, China or South Africa. I'll still have my sausages, rashers, meat and chicken until something more exciting or better foods are on the table that I know where they come from.

Chapter 72

Will our plan to save the world ever work?

In recent years a new breed of save the world volunteers have appeared on the horizon. A lot of their ideas don't always work. In fairness a lot of them would work if they got a hearing from governments around the world. Politicians love to talk about doing things but seldom have the interest in taking it any further because there may be a bit of work and thinking involved.

Last month I visited a landfill site to see the amount of waste we dump. It was unbelievable the number of plastic bottles, plastic packaging and other useless packaging that should never be used to wrap anything. A few years ago, some genius came up with the idea that we put a levy on plastic bags to try to eliminate plastic bags. It didn't work. You probably don't know why it didn't work because you were never told.

At the time the levy was put on plastic bags you could get a paper bag in many shops for your fruit and vegetables and groceries. So, the levy on plastic bags did work. The government took in over €5 million in 2017 on plastic bag charges. That wasn't really a levy. The retailer bought the plastic bag, charged the 70c levy and gave the levy to the government. So, it was a win, win. It did little to stop people using plastic bags, but what it did was it got rid of paper bags that we all used to use. Since then suppliers have got around the levy because you now buy onions, bananas and apples in plastic bags. There is no levy on this plastic packaging because the bananas are packed into plastic in South Africa or Columbia. So, what is the solution to our plastic bags over supply? Ban the use of single use plastic bags across the world. We could set the example here in Ireland.

This move could create thousands of jobs worldwide because we could grow more trees to make paper bags and we could cut down on oil consumption which plays puck with the ozone layer because plastic is a by-product of oil. So, the sales in oil might drop if we go into the forests for timber. In a way we don't know where we are going because we don't know what we want in life, to save the planet or save ourselves.

Last summer a neighbour of mine was burning a few dry branches in his back garden and he was approached by a council official and threatened with prosecution for burning. In the house 100 yards away, he had a solid fuel wood burning stove and a solid fuel barbecue in the garden which complied with Irish burning laws even though he was using the same fuel. It's a bit of a mystery what this 'Burn Deal' and 'No Burn Deal' is about. In fairness the fire in his back garden which was in a barrel could spread to neighbours' bogs and cause a lot of damage to property and a serious threat to life. I don't think that's why Ireland has a 'No Burn Deal' in place. It's mainly down to the fact that some sorts of burning cause holes in the ozone layer in the same way when cows and horses fart. I think we have a lot further to go to get to the bottom of it.

One of the greatest scourges to our planet is batteries. The sale of batteries has increased by over 100 percent in two decades. They are full of quare stuff that plays havoc with the earth and the ozone layer with acid and other stuff leaking out of batteries. Acid has been proven to be bad for you even though we all have it in our stomachs. Obviously, that type of acid you cannot use to make batteries. In fairness we have come a long way in the recycling of batteries but there are millions of them dumped into landfill every year. The sale of batteries is expected to more than double over the next ten years because of the number of electric cars coming on the market.

Social media has put an end to many people's social life. Cheap off-licence drink has put an end to many people's social lives. Semiconductor chips have played puck with our ability to do things and buy things we like to buy today not tomorrow; and drink, what can I say about it? Like anything in life, if you overindulge it can have a serious effect on your health and pocket. Not for everyone, only those who cannot handle it in a moderate, modest fashion.

Work they say is the curse of the working class. Over the years I met and knew people who never worked a day in their lives. Some went to work nearly every day except the days they took off sick to play golf or just because they did enough to justify the ways they were paid. There were others who were born retired. There was never a job that suited them or they were never suited to work. This was often referred to as being allergic to work (ATW).

For a number of years, I used to regularly meet one of these characters sitting on a windowsill observing the world. I would greet him by saying 'It's a great day', his response was as he sat in a string vest, the arms folded up smoking a fag, 'It's a great day Oliver, do you know if I was working today, I would nearly take the day off'.

Over the years I always looked for new ideas and new ways of doing things simpler. If I came up with an idea, I stuck with it until I got it right and I then ran with it. Sometimes I spent a lot of time chasing a loser. When that happened, I put it on the back burner and revisited at a later date, I might have changed my formula and ran with it again. I only gave up when I realised that this brilliant plan I have was costing me a lot of money and was going nowhere so I threw in the towel.

I never admitted failure. I would just say to myself and others who asked me about my brilliant idea that I was a bollox to have even tried it in the first place. Then again if you don't try things in life, you may miss out on a lot. These things didn't happen like this too often and I have no regrets for trying.

Chapter 73

Regrets, I've had a few

Most of us have regrets in life. The things we should have done. The things we could have done. The money we could have made if we only knew. Oftentimes people ask me if I have any regrets in life and my answer is, 'Of course I have regrets with some of the decisions I made, especially the bad ones'. The next question I'm usually asked is if you had your life to live all over again what would you do?

My answer was and is I would live my life all over again but I might change a few things if I could. Then again everything isn't possible to achieve in life so I'm happy to settle with what I can achieve.

I made mistakes I regret, and I got opportunities that I didn't expect. They say if you never make a mistake, you never do anything.

People often ask me how I would like to be remembered. Personally, I don't really want to be remembered but I would like my family, friends and people who know me to remember the things I did in life that befitted them and they got enjoyment from. To the people I gave a lift to in life when they were down. To me that's what matters. I don't want to be remembered for the amount of money I made or lost in life. That's immaterial if you don't have a happy family life where you cause no grief to anyone or get any grief from people.

Oftentimes people are remembered for how famous they were instead of being remembered for what you did for the betterment of society.

I think what I did will be judged on what I did for society and what I gave back to society. I would hope I gave a few people a laugh which we all need to do to stay happy and focused.

When one reads of all the spectacular failures in Ireland over the years, it would have been impossible for a lot of people not to have made mistakes or lost money.

In many cases people were hoodwinked by false accounting, fake news, convincing conmen and blind eyes from reputable financial advisors. In every era these people are around. They may not be referred to as unreliable sources because, in reality, they know the law and how to use the laws better than the lawmakers.

People are regularly taken in by fraudsters, especially old, vulnerable people who are oftentimes robbed of their life savings. There are hundreds of different ways of losing money. We can be naive and part with money because we believe we are getting an unbelievable deal. We can pay way over the top for a product or a service and some people throw away money as if there was no tomorrow. I have to admit I made mistakes. To some people they could be classed as stupid mistakes; to me they are part of life that all of us may experience at some time or another.

Recently I sold shares in a company that was heralded a few years ago as a company of the future because of the business they operated in. There was word around that you couldn't lose out if you bought their shares, even without first doing your sums and using your own gut instinct, even though you may get both of those wrong.

I fell for the hype and bought shares in Kenmare Resources. I invested €7,000 some years ago in the hope of making a killing, whether I made the killing or not I wasn't going to have any hang ups about it. Obviously, I would regret buying them if I knew I wouldn't get my €7,000 back. Earlier this year I sold them for €280, a loss of €6,720 plus the charges the stockbroker added on over eight years. It wasn't the end of the world. It was the end of my €7,000. Then again if you are a dairy farmer, you may go out one morning and find a prized cow dead in the field and there is nothing you can do about it.

Kenmare Resources is a public company, with a host of subsidiaries, listed on the UK stock market. Ten years ago, the company was valued at nearly €2 billion, today it's valued at €317 million with a turnover of €141 million in 2016 and they made a loss of €25 million. The company is still going because some investors still see a future in the titanium mine they own in northern Mozambique. Whether this will ever come to anything is anyone's guess. Anyway, I got out with the princely loss of over €7,000.

Kenmare's woes have been well documented over the years by various commentators. It's a bit like the banking woes. That's the gamble you take with the stock market.

We saw some of the great names in Ireland who we all believed would last forever producing crystal, glass, selling insurance, running banks and printing newspapers or drilling for the oil that never gushed. We've seen it all and we will see it as long as people are prepared to gamble money on good and bad ideas. Money is meant to go around. It is meant to be made and lost. One person's loss is another person's gain.

Chapter 74

The final roundup

Last week I decided I would do a final roundup of my thoughts and places before we went to print. I always hated to miss out on things I may have forgotten or people I once knew who impressed me or played any positive part in my life and times.

I headed for Carrick-on-Shannon and picked up Des Keane, a man very familiar with the area where I grew up. He started off on the road selling his wares in country shops, travelling shops and huckster shops around the west of Ireland. He was, and still is, a great salesman who knew and respected his customers.

On our journey for our world tour of South Leitrim he would point out the places now closed up in some country area where they had their travelling shops, a shop on the roadside selling everything from nails to horseshoes, meal for cattle, coffins and everything you needed to live life and everything to send you off, like bottles of stout, whiskey and snuff for ladies. Des supplied many products for schools like books, folders, pencils, ink and chalk for the children. For the ladies he sold 'nylons' which were later replaced with 'tights'. For the menfolk he sold razor blades, stockings, long johns, wellingtons, soap and other fancy stuff.

Des was often referred to as 'the fellow who covered the arses of the masses and the legs of the lassies' because his two biggest selling lines to shops were men's underwear and ladies' nylons.

In the 20 minutes it took us to get to our first port of call I thought I was writing Des's memoirs instead of my own.

We pulled up at Fox's Pub in Tooman for refreshments. From there we headed past Paddy Kelly's. Paddy was our postman. He was a regular visitor in Fox's Pub on his daily round. Paddy was a brainy, contrary little man, when you raised his temper. I used to call to his little home to listen to those quare stories he would have picked up on his rounds or the stories he often read on postcards he used to deliver. He always had a problem with the 'draw' in the chimney. The house was always full of smoke because he seldom cleaned it. Paddy had a dog called 'Sooner'. A quare name for a dog. I asked him one day why he called the dog 'Sooner'. He said it was because, 'He would sooner shite in the house than go outside'. He probably saw his master use his newly fitted house toilet and he felt he had to obey his master. Dogs have brains too, many of them are more tuned in than their two legged friends. Paddy's house is long since gone, replaced by a modern four bedroom bungalow and Paddy has long since gone to his eternal reward. He certainly deserved it.

Next we were heading over the whinny roads towards Ballinamuck. It was on this road where my father's people came from. They farmed about 60 acres at the top and bottom of Pod's Hill. The farm and family were known as Pod Colreavy's because every second family was a Colreavy. My folks lived in Pod's Lane which was about half a mile long. We drove in the lane that was once alive with horses, carts, men and women going to the bog or heading to the hayfields. There were nine houses in Pod's Lane. Today they are all gone except for a new one built in recent times by Albert Clarke who now lives in New York, but the family come back here every year on vacation. The Lane is now somewhat overgrown with briars, bushes, whins and wildflowers. All the nine houses were on the left side of the road. I'm not sure if the planning laws were the same nearly 200 years ago as they are today where you might not be allowed to build on the right hand side of the road.

One of the reasons all the houses were on the left side of the road was because there was a famine graveyard on the right hand side of the road. The old house foundations and stones are the only thing that's visible now and the mounds of clay over the graves are there, no headstones or markings over any of them. Some say that these graves may also be graves of young people who died from hunger or the Spanish Flu over 100 years ago. Today my ancestors' land is divided and a big part of it makes up the Gaelic pitch and building in Gortletteragh.

From here I head just a half mile over the road towards Drumlish where relations of mine were born and reared in this area in a place called Drumshanbo South. This part of Leitrim is well populated because most of the young people of today built their homes on the family farm beside their siblings like the Quinns. Many of the Quinns either work in the area or moved to America, where you will find one or two of them in and around New York. They were all very much into sport and one of them, Séamus Quinn, was the first Leitrim man to win an All-Star award with Leitrim when they qualified for the All-Ireland semi-final in 1993. Further up the road we came to the Longford/Leitrim border. We passed by Drumshanbo School which was built in 1898 and closed just 50 years later in 1948. The school turned out some go ahead people who excelled in many walks of life. Most of the houses in this area, which is known as the Black Sticks, are now closed or gone.

From where I stood here on the Longford/Leitrim border, I could see the homes of three successful people who never went past the national school in Drumshanbo South. John Griffin, Eddie Bohan and Tom Magee all went on to become multi-millionaires in Dublin and London.

Next, we headed back towards Sorohan's Pub in Cornageeha. Des remembered calling there in the '70s and selling Mick Sorohan eight dozen pairs of nylons, a scatter of razor blades and stockings for the men on the bog. Then we were on our way to the neighbouring parish of Aughavas. Aughavas was a bit like Gortletteragh. A lot of hills, lakes, rivers, mountains, swamps and good land that was hard to manage because it was so hilly. In many fields you could not use a tractor or horse to plough because of the hills. Most farmers had to make ridges for the potatoes with a 'loy'. Despite the fact that many had to emigrate because of small holdings and big families, it didn't stop their 'drive and initiative'. In one small area of Aughavas they produced six multi-millionaires in just two houses.

The Quinns of Rossan ran the local country shop. When I was a young fella, I used to visit Rossan. Odie, the homeboy who came to work in our house to 'mind' me, had previously lived and worked in Paddy Nichols in Rossan just down the road from Quinns shop. I used to meet the bread van every morning outside Quinns shop and get my hot cross buns with the money Odie gave me from his pension.

Paddy Nichols' house was where I spent many happy summers on the bog with Odie. What I liked most about it was there was a shop that sold all the stuff I liked. Paddy was a good musician and he later went on to set up a band with Mick Flavin.

The Quinn family moved on and the shop eventually closed. Three of the family went into various businesses and became very successful. They became multi-millionaires and still never forget their roots or their upbringing. Joe Quinn went on to own Galco Steel and Sperrin Metal. His brother, Frank Quinn owned the International Meat Company in Grand Canal Street in Dublin and Leixlip. Another brother, P Quinn, went on to establish Quinnsworth in Longford along with a number of other successful businesses. To me in my young years these people were an inspiration when I went to work in Quinnsworth after I left college having failed in my efforts to become a priest.

Down the road from Quinns of Rossan was the McGovern family. They were reared on a small holding so for most of the family the only option was emigration. Many of them headed to London where Peter McGovern went into the pub trade. He ran and owned the iconic Crown Pub in Cricklewood in London for many years. His brother Tony went into the construction business and now operates a huge waste disposal and skip hire business in London.

Their brother James McGovern, whom I had known for many years, bought a pub in Edgeworthstown in Longford in the late '60s. I remember he told me that he had sold the pub in the '70s for £17,000 and he had bought a pub in Dublin for £27,000. I was shocked at the price he had given. I said, 'Are you mad? why would you give £10,000 more for a pub in Dublin?' His answer was simple, 'There is more noise on the streets of Dublin than there is here'. A good logical answer. Despite that situation in the '70s, pubs everywhere nowadays are struggling to survive because of the drink at home culture in Ireland and across the world.

Sadly, Peter and James McGovern have passed away. The famous Dublin pub 'The Goblet' on Malahide Road is now run by James's family and thriving after many major extensions to it over the years.

Travelling anywhere around Ireland we see vast changes everywhere. Gone are the friendly neighbours standing at the door to greet you as you pass. You could travel for miles without seeing anyone. Are we all obsessed with mobile devices, Snapchat, Facebook and Twitter? Are these our new friends? Is Alexa the only one you can ask a question off and be sure to get an answer? There is no point in trying to have a conversation with someone who is sending text messages to someone else. That's the way forward whether we like it or not.

From Aughavas I head back to the new highway they built from Dublin to Castlebar. But before I do, I have one more port of call. I pass through Gortletteragh again and check out the home where John Hart lived in Clooncoose.

John Hart didn't spend long in the drains on his father's farm down the road from my home. John went to school with my grandfather but emigrated to Canada when he was just 19 years old and ten years later, he owned his own finance company. That was only the beginning of a remarkable career and life.

He entered political life in 1916, elected to a provincial legislature for British Colombia as a member of the Liberal group. He served as Minister for Finance in British Columbia from 1917-1924 and again from 1933 to 1947. He had retired from 1924-33 to attend to his business. He became Premier of British Columbia in 1941, serving as the highest ranking politician in the vast Canadian province for six years.

One of the programmes he was particularly remembered for was a substantial programme of rural electrification. Coming from where he did in Leitrim, it is not surprising that he understood its importance. He retired as Premier in 1947 of his own accord and became Speaker after that before standing down from politics ahead of the 1949 election.

In William Rayner's book on British Columbia premiers, titled *Premiers in Profile – The Good, The Bad and The Transient*, Rayner said 'Hart may have been the best minister of finance British Columbia ever had'.

Journalist Bruce Hutchison was very impressed by Hart's role as premier. "He is unexcitable and he is giving us a new brand of quiet, unheroic government which is certainly the most competent and honest we have had within 25 years of this reporter's intimate experience," he wrote in 1945.

I think Ireland's loss was Canada's gain.

Money as a rule won't make your life much happier while you are here. It can create a lot of problems after you leave here depending on who gets their hands on the money. I was never obsessed with money. I was more obsessed with being a success at what I put my mind down to do. I would hate to be remembered as a failure. I would hate to be remembered as someone who wanted to have more money and wealth than any of my friends. I would hate to be remembered as a non-caring person who felt the world belonged to me and how I would tell everyone else how they should live their lives.

Unfortunately, in the new world, we have a lot of these types of people around who are obsessed with money and your money, as if they were planning to bring it with them. You're better to be remembered for what good you did in life as against being remembered for the amount of money you left after you.

A typical example was the late Steve Jobs who created Apple. He is remembered for what he gave the world, not for the amount of money he made in this world. Many people in the modern world are obsessed with power and money regardless of how much power and money they have. Oftentimes these types of people are difficult to understand or have a real conversation with. The good thing about that is that everyone in the world is not like that, which is good for us all.

That to me was one of the advantages of living and growing up in rural Ireland. Most of my neighbours I knew who made it good in the world of business never changed much because of the success and wealth they created. They did well in life and business because they still were nice, decent people who didn't forget their roots. Many of these people who went to America or England sent money back to their families to help them in life because many who stayed on the small holding of land in the west were less fortunate. We were all lucky to live in a country with that culture. These people bailed out the country at a time when we had no money or banks who would lend money.

Today things have changed a bit because for the past 15 years all of us have been bailing out the banks, the builders and the government and they still cannot get it right. Maybe it's time we gave them time to accumulate money themselves so we can pay off the billions we owe with money we can or could accumulate from all the great resources we have surrounding us on land and in the seas.

You could say a lot of people nowadays act like Odie did. He could bail me out anytime my finances were depleted. He never asked if I squandered the money or spent it wisely and I didn't do any financial reports for him for obvious reasons. Some things haven't changed much and if Odie was bailing out the government then, he probably wouldn't get any explanation as to how they squandered his money.

The new generation with new AI technology will change all this and we may end up as the wealthiest little country in the world again.

Chapter 75

My plans from here

I was bitten by the travel bug many years ago. It's the hardest bug to shake off. In the next few weeks, I am planning a world tour of Mayo, Sligo and Leisfriends a couple of days. After that I'm planning to visit Australia for a few weeks to recap on the scenes around the world. Maybe hire out a motorbike and tour the county. Maybe look into Tasmania to see the fate of some of the Irish who were banished to Van Diemen's Land for crimes you would now get a telling off from a judge for.

I might travel to New Zealand. The home of Pink Lady apples and see how they can rear over 23 million sheep every year and ship the meat to every part of the world. I might even spend a few days in Bangladesh to see how they can produce billions of tee shirts and underpants to cover the bare arses and bellies of the world.

Maybe I might stop off in Italy to see how our Pope is getting on or head on for Germany and see how they are cooking a bit for themselves and keeping themselves warm now that Russia has scuttled their gas supplies.

On the way back, I might even drop into Westminster to tell them about the big mistake they made by abandoning their saviours whom they paid £100 billion to for the pleasure of being a member of the EU. There is no comeback now.

On my way back to Ireland I will need to buy myself warm clothes and an umbrella to be ready for the Irish weather. It will be summer in Australia when I arrive there and when I leave there. It will be winter in Ireland.

It's a strange world that's a bit upside down. Today and next week it's downside up. There is nothing much we can do about that until the scientists sort that one out. For now, I'm going to have to put up with my lot, hope for the best and hope we will all be around for a while, living a happy, good life that hopefully nobody or nothing will take away from us.

On my return I hope all of you good people will have read my book and you will be in a position to give me expert advice on how I organised my life and times. Should I have done things differently to better myself? Should I have become a professor or a scientist and save the world?

Or should I have taken one of the first pieces of serious advice my father gave me, 'AND STAYED IN THE DRAIN?'